Keys to Paradise: Serving Parents with Excellence

Forty Hadiths on Honoring and Respecting Parents

Aisha Othman, Esquire

To my beloved parents,

who were my first teachers, guiding me with their love, wisdom, and patience. Though you are no longer with me in this world, your sacrifices, prayers, and unwavering support continue to shape who I am today. This book is a small token of my endless gratitude for all that you have given me. May Allah envelop you in His mercy and grant you the highest place in Jannah.

To all the mothers and fathers,

whose love knows no bounds and whose sacrifices often go unseen. May this collection inspire your children to honor you as you deserve, and may your kindness and dedication be rewarded in both this life and the Hereafter.

And to every child,

who seeks the pleasure of Allah by striving to fulfill the rights of their parents. May these Hadiths guide your journey toward being the best version of yourself for those who have nurtured and raised you.

With love, gratitude, and hope,

Aisha Othman

Copyright © 2024 by Aisha Othman

Email: darannoor1@gmail.com

All rights reserved. No part of this book may be reproduced, distributed, or transmitted in any form or by any means, including photocopying, recording, or other electronic or mechanical methods, without the prior written permission of the publisher or author, except in the case of brief quotations embodied in critical reviews and certain other non-commercial uses permitted by U.S. copyright law.

This publication is intended to provide accurate and authoritative information regarding the subject matter presented. It is distributed with the understanding that neither the author nor the publisher is engaged in providing legal, financial, accounting, or other professional services. While every effort has been made to ensure the accuracy of the content, the author and publisher make no representations or warranties regarding the completeness or accuracy of the information contained within. The advice and strategies outlined in this book may not be applicable to your individual situation. It is recommended that you seek professional guidance as needed.

Neither the author nor the publisher shall be liable for any loss of profit, personal or business damages, or any other form of commercial loss, including special, incidental, or consequential damages, arising from the use or reliance upon the information contained in this book.

First edition, 2024

Contents

Preface	XI
Introduction	1
1. Earning Allah's Pleasure Through Parents	4

    Hadith 1: The Path to Allah's Pleasure and Displeasure: Through the Treatment of Parents

    Hadith 2: The Best of Deeds: Praying on Time and Honoring Parents

    Hadith 3: Parents: The Gateway to Paradise Through Honor and Obedience

    Hadith 4: The Best of Deeds: Prayer, Dutifulness to Parents, and Striving in Allah's Cause

2. The Rewards of Serving and Honoring Parents   10

    Hadith 5: Blessings of Sustenance and Longevity Through Maintaining Family Ties

    Hadith 6: Dutifulness to Parents is a Shield From Hellfire

3. The High Status of Mothers   14

    Hadith 7: The Precedence of a Mother's Rights: A Threefold Emphasis on Maternal Honor

    Hadith 8: Paradise Lies Beneath a Mother's Feet: The Priority of Serving One's Mother Over Jihad

4. Serving Parents with Love and Dedication   17
    Hadith 9: The Unrepayable Debt to Mothers: Sacrifices Beyond Comparison
    Hadith 10: The Incomparable Debt to Fathers: A Child's Duty of Gratitude and Service

5. Honoring and Dutifulness to Parents Even After Their Death   24
    Hadith 11: The Benefit of Charity on Behalf of a Deceased Parent: Saad ibn Ubadah's Gift for His Mother
    Hadith 12: Three Ongoing Sources of Reward After Death: Charity, Knowledge, and Righteous Offspring
    Hadith 13: Fulfilling Vows for Deceased Parents: A Daughter's Duty to Complete Her Mother's Fast
    Hadith 14: Honoring Parents After Death: Acts of Righteousness to Benefit Deceased Parents

6. Respecting Parents Even if They Are Non-Muslim   31
    Hadith 15: Maintaining Ties with Non-Muslim Parents: The Prophet's Guidance to Asma bint Abu Bakr
    Hadith 16: Kindness to Non-Muslim Parents: The Prophet's Command to Honor Mothers

7. Protecting Parental Honor   36
    Hadith 17: The Grave Sin of Cursing One's Parents Through Indirect Abuse

8. Being Kind and Gentle to Parents   39
    Hadith 18: The Duty of Humility and Mercy Toward Parents: A Qur'anic Command (Quran 17:24)
    Hadith 19: The Greatest of Major Sins: Shirk and Disobedience to Parents

9. The Importance of Patience and Forbearance with Parents — 43
   Hadith 20: The Path to Paradise: Fulfilling the Rights of Allah and Parents
   Hadith 21: Parental Rights Over Wealth: 'You and Your Wealth Belong to Your Father

Book Review Request — 48

10. Honoring Parents in Their Old Age — 49
    Hadith 22: The Disgrace of Neglecting Elderly Parents: A Missed Opportunity for Paradise
    Hadith 23: The Reward of Caring for Elderly Parents: Under Allah's Shade on the Day of Judgment

11. Respect for Parent's Wishes — 53
    Hadith 24: The Pleasure of Allah Lies in Parental Obedience: A Call to Sacrifice for Parents' Satisfaction
    Hadith 25: Parental Authority and Personal Choices: The Duty of Obeying Parents in Marital Decisions

12. Supplicating for Parents — 59
    Hadith 26: The Elevation of a Parent's Status in Paradise Through a Child's Prayers
    Hadith 27: Dutifulness After Death: Honoring Parents by Maintaining Their Relationships and Praying for Them

13. The Impact of Treating Parents Well on Children's Lives — 64
    Hadith 28: The Blessings of Sustenance and Longevity Through Upholding Family Ties
    Hadith 29: The Reciprocal Blessing of Kindness to Parents

14. The Grave Sin of Disobedience to Parents — 68
    Hadith 30: The Gravest of Major Sins: Shirk and Disobedience to Parents
    Hadith 31: Three Prayers Never Rejected: The Oppressed, the Traveler, and the Parent Against Their Child

Hadith 32: Three Sins That Bring Immediate Punishment: Disobedience to Parents, Injustice, and Ingratitude

Hadith 33: Three People Deprived of Allah's Mercy on the Day of Judgment

15. Maintaining Good Relations with Parents' Friends and Relatives   73

Hadith 34: Honoring Family Legacy: The Righteousness of Kindness to a Father's Friends

Hadith 35: The Highest Form of Goodness: Maintaining Ties with a Father's Friends After His Death

Hadith 36: The Divine Protection of Kinship Ties: A Promise of Blessing or Severance

16. Giving Charity on Behalf of Deceased Parents   78

Hadith 37: Charity for a Deceased Parent: The Continuing Benefit of Acts of Kindness

Hadith 38: Posthumous Charity: A Mother's Reward Through Her Child's Giving

17. The Influence of Parents' Supplications   82

Hadith 39: Three Supplications Always Answered: The Oppressed, the Traveler, and the Parent's Du'a for Their Child

Hadith 40: A Father's Du'a: As Powerful as a Prophet's Supplication for His People

18. The Role of Parents in Leading Children to Righteousness   88

Hadith 41: Responsibility of Leadership: Every Individual is a Shepherd of Their Own Flock

Hadith 42: The Greatest Gift: A Father's Legacy of Good Manners

Hadith 43: Excellence Begins at Home: The Best Among You Are Best to Their Families

19. Honoring and Treating Parents with Excellence in the Quran   95

    1. Surah Al-Isra (17:23-24)

    2. Surah Luqman (31:14-15)

3. Surah Al-Ankabut (29:8)

4. Surah Al-Ahqaf (46:15)

5. Surah Al-An'am (6:151)

6. Surah Maryam (19:14-15) - About Prophet Yahya (John)

7. Surah Maryam (19:32) - About Prophet Isa

20. Acts of Kindness Toward Parents: Inspiring Examples from Early Muslims   100

    1. Uwais al-Qarni: A Model of Devotion

    2. Abdullah ibn Umar: Reverence After Death

    3. Abu Huraira: Carrying His Mother

    4. Ali ibn Abi Talib: Respecting Fatimah bint Asad

    5. Zain ul-Abidin: The Pious Son of Hussain ibn Ali

21. Kindness to Parents: Exemplary Stories from Later Generations of Muslims   104

    1. Imam Abu Hanifa: Serving His Mother with Dedication

    2. Rabi'a al-Adawiyya: Dutifulness to Parents and Elevated Spiritual Status

    3. Imam Al-Shafi'i: Honoring His Mother

    4. Muhammad ibn Sirin: Exceptional Kindness to His Mother

    5. Sufyan Al-Thawri: Prioritizing His Mother's Needs

    6. Fudayl ibn Iyad: From a Life of Sin to Elevated Spiritual Status Through Filial Devotion

    7. Yahya ibn Muadh Al-Razi: Carrying Out His Mother's Desires

22. Kindness to Parents: Notable Examples from Contemporary Islamic Scholars   109

    1. Mufti Taqi Usmani: Prioritizing His Parents' Well-Being

    2. Shaykh Muhammad Mukhtar al-Shinqiti: Humility Before His Mother

    3. Shaykh Bin Bayyah: Compassionate Care for His Father

23. The Story of Jurayj, the Devoted Worshipper   112

24. Lives of the Hadith Narrators: Biographical Insights   115
    1. Imams of Kutub al-Sittah (the six canonical hadith collections in Sunni Islam)
    2. Other Narrators of Hadiths

Conclusion   123

End Book Review Request   125

References   126

Preface

In the Name of Allah, the Most Gracious, the Most Merciful. Praise be to Allah, the Lord of all worlds, and may peace and blessings be upon His final Messenger, Muhammad, his family, his companions, and all those who follow his path until the Day of Judgment.

The love and respect that Islam commands toward one's parents is unparalleled. From the moment a child is born to the later stages of life, a parent's role in nurturing, caring, and guiding their offspring is one of the greatest manifestations of sacrifice and devotion. Islam emphasizes this relationship as a pillar of moral and social conduct. In an age where familial bonds are often strained, there is a need to revisit the timeless teachings of our Prophet Muhammad (peace and blessings be upon him) regarding parents and to understand how fulfilling this duty brings us closer to Allah and ultimately to Paradise.

This book, ***Keys to Paradise: Serving Parents with Excellence —Forty Hadiths on Honoring and Respecting Parents***, is inspired by both the teachings of the Prophet (peace and blessings be upon him) and a significant hadith found in **Imam Nawawi's collection of forty Hadiths**, which states, "Whoever preserves for my people forty Hadiths concerning their religion, Allah will raise him as a scholar on the Day of Resurrection." This hadith motivated generations of scholars to compile collections of forty Hadiths on various topics, each aimed at preserving and transmitting essential knowledge to benefit the Ummah (Muslim community).

With this tradition in mind, I sought to compile a collection of forty Hadiths specifically focused on the excellence of treating parents with kindness and respect. The relationship with our parents is a key aspect of faith, and it is through understanding and applying Prophetic guidance on this matter that we can unlock the doors to Jannah (Paradise). The title of this book, **Keys to Paradise**, reflects the recurring message in these Hadiths: that treating one's parents well is one of the most direct and powerful ways to attain Allah's pleasure and secure eternal bliss.

Each Hadith in this collection is followed by a brief explanation to clarify its meaning and help readers reflect on how they can apply these teachings. The Hadiths are also categorized into themes that reflect different aspects of parental honor: the status of mothers, the duties of caring for parents in old age, the consequences of neglect, and the continuous responsibility to pray for parents after their passing.

My motivation in writing this book stems from my desire to contribute to this noble tradition and personal reflection on my parents' profound impact on my life. As they have both passed away, this work is also a form of honoring their memory and seeking to benefit them through good deeds. I hope this book will inspire others to reflect on their relationships with their parents, seek forgiveness where necessary, and commit to treating them with the reverence and love that leads to the highest station in the Hereafter.

I want to thank the scholars and teachers whose work has guided me in compiling these Hadiths. I ask Allah to accept this humble effort and make it beneficial for all who read it. May Allah, the Exalted, grant us the strength and sincerity to honor our parents and attain His pleasure and Paradise through that. Ameen.

All praise is due to Allah, Lord of the Worlds. If this work is successful, it is due to Allah's generosity; if there are mistakes, they are from my shortcomings. I ask Allah to guide and protect me and my family, for He supports those who rely on Him. I seek Allah's forgiveness for my shortcomings and pray for His blessings of well-being and success in this world and the next.

Aisha Othman
October 2024

INTRODUCTION

The bond between parents and children is one of the most sacred relationships that Islam holds in high esteem. Rooted in love, respect, and mercy, the parent-child dynamic is a cornerstone of Islamic morality and spirituality. In the Qur'an, Allah reminds us of the significance of honoring our parents, often coupling this command with the obligation to worship Him alone. This emphasis is not coincidental but rather a reflection of the divine order of relationships: worshiping Allah and respecting our parents are foundational to a believer's journey to success in this world and the Hereafter.

Islamic teachings emphasize that parents are a means through which we can attain Allah's pleasure and, ultimately, Jannah (Paradise). The guidance of the Prophet Muhammad (peace and blessings be upon him) is filled with examples of parents' high status, the rewards for treating them well, and the severe consequences of neglecting their rights. Parental honor is described as a direct path to Jannah, where the pleasure of Allah is intimately tied to the pleasure of one's parents.

This book, ***Keys to Paradise: Serving Parents with Excellence —Forty Hadiths on Honoring and Respecting Parents***, is a humble attempt to present the timeless guidance of our beloved Prophet (peace and blessings be upon him) on the subject of parental respect and care. The focus on "Forty Hadiths" follows a noble tradition in Islamic scholarship, where scholars compile concise collections on a particular topic, making it easier for believers to internalize and act upon the teachings. Each Hadith included in this book has been carefully selected to highlight various aspects of parental excellence: the obligation of honoring parents, the rights of mothers, the consequences of disrespect, and the ongoing responsibilities toward parents even after their passing.

Why focus on parents in particular? Because parents, by Allah's command, hold one of the highest stations in our lives. From the sacrifices of a mother who bore us in difficulty to the guidance and protection of a father, our existence and well-being are intertwined with their love and care. The Prophet Muhammad (peace and blessings be upon him) consistently urged his followers to treat their parents with the utmost kindness and gentleness, regardless of the challenges that may arise. As the demands of modern life often pull us away from familial responsibilities, this book seeks to remind us that one of the most accessible and direct paths to Jannah lies within the walls of our homes—in how we treat our parents.

The Hadiths in this collection are categorized to allow for an easy and systematic understanding of parental rights in Islam. Beginning with the importance of honoring parents, moving through the responsibilities toward them during their lifetime and after their death, and addressing the consequences of disrespect, this book provides both spiritual and practical guidance. Each Hadith is followed by a brief explanation to provide clarity and context, allowing readers to appreciate the depth of these Prophetic teachings fully.

In a world where values are often shifting, where the elderly are sometimes neglected, and where the family unit faces new challenges, Islam offers a blueprint for navigating these complexities with compassion and integrity. By revisiting these sacred teachings, we are reminded that our path to Paradise is not distant or unattainable—it begins with those closest to us, our parents. Honoring them is an act of gratitude and a divine obligation that opens the doors to spiritual elevation and eternal reward.

I invite you, dear reader, to reflect deeply on these Hadiths, to contemplate your relationship with your parents, and to implement these teachings in your daily life. May this collection serve as a reminder, a source of inspiration, and a guide toward fulfilling one of the most important duties Allah has placed upon us: honoring our parents and securing our place among those blessed with the keys to Paradise.

Chapter 1

Earning Allah's Pleasure Through Parents

Hadith 1: The Path to Allah's Pleasure and Displeasure: Through the Treatment of Parents

Narrated by Abdullah ibn Amr (may Allah be pleased with him): The Prophet (peace and blessings be upon him) said: "The pleasure of Allah lies in the pleasure of the parents, and the anger of Allah lies in the anger of the parents." (Jami` at-Tirmidhi, Book 27, Hadith 1899)

Key Lessons

1. **Connection Between Parental Pleasure and Allah's Pleasure**: This hadith establishes that a person's relationship with their parents mirrors their relationship with Allah. Pleasing one's parents brings Allah's pleasure, and angering them invites His displeasure, illustrating the spiritual impact of one's treatment of one's parents.

2. **Parental Rights as a Divine Duty**: The connection made between Allah's pleasure and the parents' highlights that obedience and respect

toward parents are fundamental aspects of one's relationship with Allah, and they must be prioritized to attain His favor.

Hadith 2: The Best of Deeds: Praying on Time and Honoring Parents

Narrated by Ibn Umar (may Allah be pleased with him): The Prophet (peace and blessings be upon him) said: "The best deeds are to perform the prayers on time and to be dutiful to one's parents." (Sahih Muslim, Hadith 85).

Key Lessons

1. **The Importance of Timely Prayers**: This hadith emphasizes the central role of **prayers (Salah)** in Islam. Performing the five daily prayers on time is regarded as one of a Muslim's best deeds. It underscores the significance of punctuality in Salah, highlighting that it is not just the act of praying but the timely fulfillment of this obligation that earns greater reward. Praying on time demonstrates discipline, devotion, and a commitment to maintaining a strong connection with Allah.

2. **Dutifulness to Parents as a Top Priority**: Right after timely prayers, **being dutiful to one's parents** is mentioned as one of the best deeds in Islam. This emphasizes the high status of parents in Islamic teachings and the importance of treating them with respect, kindness, and care. Dutifulness (*birr al-walidayn*) involves not just obedience but also caring for their well-being, fulfilling their needs, and showing them love and patience throughout their lives, especially in their old age.

3. **Balanced Relationship Between Worship and Social Responsibilities**: The combination of the two best deeds—timely prayers and dutifulness to parents—illustrates the balance Islam promotes between a person's relationship with Allah (through worship) and their relationship with people, especially their parents. Islam

encourages believers to be conscious of both their spiritual and social duties. This balance is a key part of being a well-rounded and righteous Muslim, showing that success in the Hereafter is achieved through worship and fulfilling moral responsibilities toward others.

4. **Parental Respect as a Form of Worship**: In Islam, being dutiful to one's parents is considered an act of worship, similar to performing Salah. The respect and care shown toward parents are seen as a direct means to earn Allah's pleasure. Neglecting parents or failing to fulfill their rights is viewed as a grave sin. This hadith teaches that one's devotion to Allah is reflected in how one treats one's parents, making kindness and respect toward them a critical element of a Muslim's character.

5. **Prioritizing Responsibilities**: By listing these two actions as the best deeds, the Prophet (peace and blessings be upon him) guides Muslims in prioritizing responsibilities in their lives. This hadith teaches that performing obligatory acts of worship (such as Salah) and maintaining family ties—especially with parents—should be given precedence over other actions. It reminds Muslims of the importance of fulfilling religious and family obligations, both essential in attaining Allah's pleasure.

6. **Interconnection of Rights**: This hadith highlights the interconnection between the rights of Allah (*huquq Allah*) and the rights of people (*huquq al-'ibad*). Just as Allah has the right to be worshiped through prayer, parents also have rights over their children, and fulfilling these rights is a significant aspect of Islamic faith and practice.

Hadith 3: Parents: The Gateway to Paradise Through Honor and Obedience

Narrated by Abu Darda: "A parent is the middle door of Paradise; if you wish, you can lose it, or if you wish, you can protect it." (Sunan Ibn Majah, Book 37, Hadith 3663)

Key Lessons

1. **Parents as a Primary Access to Paradise**: This hadith reinforces the idea that the parent, particularly the "middle door," is the easiest and most direct route to Paradise. Treating parents with kindness and respect opens the door to spiritual success while neglecting or dishonoring them risks losing this precious opportunity.

2. **Choice of Protecting or Losing the Door**: The hadith reminds believers that their actions towards their parents can either safeguard this door to Paradise or cause them to lose it, indicating that the relationship with one's parents has direct consequences in the hereafter.

Hadith 4: The Best of Deeds: Prayer, Dutifulness to Parents, and Striving in Allah's Cause

Narrated by Abdullah ibn Mas'ud: "I asked the Prophet (peace and blessings be upon him), 'Which deed is the best?' He replied, 'To offer the prayers at their early stated fixed times.' I asked, 'What is next?' He replied, 'To be good and dutiful to your parents.' I again asked, 'What is next?' He replied, 'To participate in Jihad (fighting) in Allah's cause.'" (Sahih al-Bukhari, Book 93, Hadith 625)

Key Lessons

1. **Dutifulness to Parents Among the Best Deeds**: In this hadith,

the Prophet (peace and blessings be upon him) ranks being good and dutiful to one's parents as the second-best deed after offering prayers at their proper times, placing it even above participation in Jihad. This highlights the elevated status of parental care and respect in Islam.

2. **Prioritizing Family Care Over Other Acts of Worship**: The hadith shows that after performing one's religious duties, care and obedience to parents take precedence over even highly valued acts of worship like Jihad, demonstrating the immense value placed on filial piety.

Common Themes:

- **Parents as a Path to Paradise**: All four hadiths consistently teach that pleasing and caring for parents is a direct means of attaining Paradise. Whether described as the "best door" or the "middle door," honoring parents is portrayed as one of the most important actions for securing Allah's favor.

- Divine Pleasure Tied to Parental Treatment: Pleasing one's parents bring Allah pleasure while angering or neglecting them invites His anger. This shows parents' critical role in one's spiritual journey and relationship with Allah.

- **Filial Piety as a Top Priority in Islam**: Being dutiful to parents is repeatedly ranked among Islam's highest and most virtuous deeds. It is prioritized over other acts of worship and is considered one of the greatest acts a Muslim can perform.

Key Takeaways:

- **Respect and Dutifulness to Parents Are a Key to Paradise**: The hadiths make clear that honoring, pleasing, and caring for parents are essential for spiritual success and attaining Paradise. Failing in this duty can result in the loss of this opportunity.

- Parental Treatment Reflects One's Relationship with Allah: How one treats one's parents directly affects one's standing with Allah, making this a fundamental aspect of faith and worship.

- **Priority of Family Care**: These teachings emphasize the importance of being dutiful to parents, even above other significant religious acts, showing that family care is central to Islamic ethics and spirituality.

In conclusion, the hadiths emphasize the central role of parents in a Muslim's spiritual journey, highlighting that honoring, pleasing, and being dutiful to one's parents is a direct path to attaining Paradise. The relationship with parents is not only a moral obligation but also deeply connected to one's relationship with Allah, as pleasing them brings Allah's pleasure, while angering them results in His displeasure. These teachings consistently prioritize the care and respect of parents as one of the highest forms of worship, placing it above even other significant religious duties. Ultimately, a believer's treatment of their parents plays a crucial role in their success hereafter, underscoring filial piety's profound importance in Islam.

Chapter 2

The Rewards of Serving and Honoring Parents

Hadith 5: Blessings of Sustenance and Longevity Through Maintaining Family Ties

Narrated by Anas ibn Malik (may Allah be pleased with him): The Prophet (peace and blessings be upon him) said: "Whoever wishes to have his provision increased or his life prolonged should maintain good relations with his parents and relatives." (Sahih al-Bukhari, Hadith 5985)

Key Lessons

1. **Worldly Benefits of Maintaining Family Ties**: This hadith demonstrates that maintaining good relationships with parents and relatives leads to tangible, worldly benefits, such as increased provision and a longer life. Islam encourages positive familial relationships not only for spiritual reasons but also for the benefits they bring in this world.

2. **Importance of Family Bonds**: The emphasis on parents and relatives

in this hadith shows that Islam places great value on family connections. Maintaining these ties is seen as a form of worship and a means to secure both material and spiritual blessings.

3. **Holistic View of Well-being**: The hadith reflects Islam's holistic approach to well-being. It teaches that by fulfilling one's responsibilities toward parents and relatives, a person can experience blessings in their wealth and health, underscoring the connection between moral behavior and worldly success.

Hadith 6: Dutifulness to Parents is a Shield From Hellfire

Narrated by Mu'adh ibn Jabal (may Allah be pleased with him): The Prophet (peace and blessings be upon him) said: "Shall I not tell you what the major sins are? Worshiping others besides Allah, disobedience to parents, and giving false testimony." (Sahih al-Bukhari, Hadith 2511)

Key Lessons

1. **Disobedience to Parents as a Major Sin**: This hadith places disobedience to parents in the same category as **shirk** (associating partners with Allah) and false testimony, highlighting its severity. Islam regards honoring and obeying parents as a foundational moral duty, and neglecting this duty is one of the gravest offenses.

2. **The Seriousness of Disobedience in Islam**: The inclusion of disobedience to parents among the major sins shows how central the treatment of parents is in the moral framework of Islam. It is not just a social or cultural expectation but a religious obligation that carries significant spiritual consequences.

3. **Respect for Parents as a Form of Worship**: Disobeying parents is considered one of the most severe sins, akin to violating the core principles of faith and justice. This hadith teaches that being kind,

respectful, and obedient to parents is an act of worship, and failing to do so can jeopardize a person's relationship with Allah.

Key Lessons from the Hadiths

1. **Maintaining Family Ties Brings Blessings**: In the first hadith, the Prophet Muhammad (peace and blessings be upon him) teaches that maintaining good relationships with parents and relatives has spiritual rewards and tangible benefits in this life, such as increased provision and prolonged life. This highlights the practical and worldly advantages of upholding family ties in Islam, showing that Islam encourages kindness and cooperation within families to foster stability and well-being.

2. **The Status of Parents in Islam**: Both hadiths emphasize the critical role of parents in Islam and the high status of maintaining good relations with them. The Prophet (peace and blessings be upon him) associates treating parents well with two of life's greatest desires—sustenance and longevity. This reflects how highly Islam values parental care and support, linking it to success in both this world and the Hereafter.

3. **Disobedience to Parents is a Major Sin**: The second hadith places disobedience to parents among the most severe sins in Islam, second only to shirk (worshiping others besides Allah). By categorizing disobedience as one of the "major sins" alongside idol worship and false testimony, the Prophet (peace and blessings be upon him) emphasizes the seriousness of failing to honor one's parents. This teaches that disregarding the rights of parents is a grave offense in the sight of Allah, with significant consequences for one's spiritual standing.

4. **Connecting Spiritual and Social Duties**: The first hadith shows that religious and social responsibilities are interconnected. Islam promotes strong family bonds as part of one's duty to Allah, and this includes looking after one's parents and maintaining ties with extended family members. By fulfilling these duties, one gains blessings in the Hereafter

and this world, reflecting the holistic nature of Islamic teachings that merge spiritual and material well-being.

5. **The Danger of False Testimony**: In addition to disobedience to parents, the second hadith highlights giving false testimony as a major sin. This indicates that Islam strongly emphasizes truthfulness and justice in personal and societal matters. It reinforces that integrity in both word and action is essential in Islamic ethics, and violating this through lies and false testimony leads to severe moral and spiritual consequences.

6. **Prioritizing Major Sins for Moral Guidance**: By listing the major sins, the second hadith guides Muslims on what actions they must strictly avoid. It underscores the hierarchy of moral and ethical principles in Islam, where worshiping Allah alone and honoring one's parents are foundational aspects of faith. Including disobedience to parents alongside other major sins reminds believers that fulfilling family obligations is not merely a social virtue but a religious duty of utmost importance.

Conclusion

These hadiths collectively teach the value of maintaining strong family relationships, particularly with parents, as a source of divine blessings, both materially and spiritually. They also warn against major sins such as disobedience to parents, associating others with Allah, and false testimony, emphasizing the need for moral integrity. Together, these teachings encourage Muslims to prioritize family obligations and truthfulness as integral components of a righteous and successful life in accordance with Islamic principles.

Chapter 3

The High Status of Mothers

Hadith 7: The Precedence of a Mother's Rights: A Threefold Emphasis on Maternal Honor

Narrated by Abu Huraira: A man came to the Prophet (peace and blessings be upon him) and said, 'O Messenger of Allah, who is most deserving of my good company?' The Prophet (peace and blessings be upon him) said, 'Your mother.' The man asked again, 'Then who?' The Prophet (peace and blessings be upon him) replied, 'Your mother.' The man asked again, 'Then who?' The Prophet (peace and blessings be upon him) said, 'Your mother.' The man asked once more, 'Then who?' The Prophet (peace and blessings be upon him) finally said, 'Your father.' (Sahih al-Bukhari, Book 78, Hadith 2; Sahih Muslim, Book 45, Hadith 2)

Key Lessons

1. **Priority of the Mother**: This hadith emphasizes the mother's exceptional status and right to be treated with kindness and respect. The fact that the Prophet (peace and blessings be upon him) mentions the mother three times before mentioning the father highlights the great

responsibility and high level of care owed to the mother.

2. **Repetition for Emphasis**: By repeating "your mother" three times, the Prophet (peace and blessings be upon him) stresses the mother's role in one's life, particularly due to the sacrifices she makes during pregnancy, childbirth, and upbringing.

3. **Respect for Both Parents**: Though the focus is on the mother, the father is also mentioned, indicating the importance of being dutiful to both parents, with the mother having a higher degree of honor.

Hadith 8: Paradise Lies Beneath a Mother's Feet: The Priority of Serving One's Mother Over Jihad

Narrated by Mu'awiyah ibn Jahimah: Jahimah came to the Prophet (peace and blessings be upon him) and said, "O Messenger of Allah, I want to go out and fight (in Jihad), and I have come to consult you." The Prophet (peace and blessings be upon him) asked, "Do you have a mother?" Jahimah replied, "Yes." The Prophet (peace and blessings be upon him) said, "Then stay with her, for Paradise is under her feet." (Musnad Ahmad, Hadith 15538; Sunan al-Nasa'i, Book 25, Hadith 3104)

Key Lessons

1. **Paradise Under the Mother's Feet**: The Prophet (peace be upon him) highlights that serving and caring for one's mother is an act that leads to Paradise. This metaphor shows the immense reward of honoring the mother and the spiritual value of fulfilling her needs.

2. **Obligation** over Voluntary Acts: Even though Jahimah wanted to participate in Jihad, which is a highly regarded act in Islam, the Prophet (peace and blessings be upon him) instructed him to stay with his mother, emphasizing that taking care of her is of greater importance and

priority, especially when she needs support.

3. **Jihad of Caring for Parents**: This hadith indicates that serving one's mother can be a form of personal Jihad, an effort that brings great reward and spiritual success, sometimes even more than other acts of worship or duty.

Common Themes:

- **The High Status of Mothers**: Both hadiths underline the special position of the mother in Islam, where being dutiful to her is directly linked to attaining Paradise and righteousness.

- **Balance Between Parents**: While the mother is given greater emphasis in these narrations, respect for both parents is essential, with the father also holding an honored position in the family structure.

- **Service to Parents as a Path to Paradise**: Caring for one's parents, especially the mother, is depicted as a pathway to spiritual success and closeness to Allah, sometimes even superseding other virtuous acts like Jihad.

In conclusion, the two hadiths highlight the profound significance of honoring and caring for one's parents, particularly the mother, in Islam. The emphasis on the mother—mentioned three times before the father—underscores her pivotal role and immense sacrifices for her children. Respecting and serving one's parents is not only a moral duty but also a spiritual act that leads to Paradise, as reflected in the metaphor of "Paradise being under the mother's feet." Furthermore, caring for parents is regarded as an act that can even take precedence over other highly esteemed actions, such as Jihad. These teachings remind us of the immense rewards and divine blessings of maintaining strong, loving relationships with our parents and fulfilling our responsibilities toward them.

Chapter 4

Serving Parents with Love and Dedication

Hadith 9: The Unrepayable Debt to Mothers: Sacrifices Beyond Comparison

Narrated by Abdullah ibn 'Umar: A man came to the Prophet (peace and blessings be upon him) and said: "I carried my mother on my back from Makkah to Madinah. Have I fulfilled her right?" The Prophet (peace and blessings be upon him) replied: "You have not even repaid her for one contraction she felt during childbirth." (Musnad Ahmad)

Key Lessons from the Hadith:

1. **The Immense Status and Rights of Mothers**:

- This hadith emphasizes the unparalleled status of mothers in Islam and highlights the immense effort and sacrifice they undergo, especially during pregnancy, childbirth, and raising children. The Prophet (peace and blessings be upon him) made it clear that even extraordinary acts of service, such as carrying one's mother over a long distance, do not equate to the pain and hardship a mother experiences during childbirth.

- It serves as a reminder of mothers' significant role and the gratitude that children owe them for their sacrifices, which are difficult to repay fully.

2. The Incomparable Sacrifice of Mothers:
- The response of the Prophet (peace be upon him) demonstrates that no matter how much a child does for their mother, they cannot fully repay her for the sacrifices she made, particularly the physical and emotional pain of childbirth and the selfless nurturing that follows.

- It reflects the uniqueness of a mother's love and devotion, which cannot be compensated through any single noble act of service.

3. Continuous Duty Towards Parents:
- This hadith teaches that dutifulness toward parents is a lifelong responsibility that requires constant effort. Children can never fully repay their parents, especially their mothers, but they are expected to honor, serve, and care for them continuously.

- Carrying his mother was noble, but the Prophet's (peace and blessings be upon him) response shows that honoring one's parents is ongoing and cannot be measured by a single act of kindness.

4. Humility in Serving Parents:
- The man's question to the Prophet (peace and blessings be upon him) reflects a sincere desire to fulfill his mother's rights. However, the Prophet's (peace and blessings be upon him) reply encourages humility in service to one's parents. No matter how great the service is, one must recognize that it is impossible to repay them, especially a mother fully.

- This hadith reminds children to serve their parents with humility, understanding that their service is a continual duty and should be done out of love and gratitude, not out of a sense of having "repaid" them.

4. The Importance of Gratitude and Compassion:

- The hadith stresses the importance of **gratitude** toward one's mother and parents in general. A mother's selfless devotion cannot be repaid by worldly deeds alone, so children should constantly show gratitude through their actions, words, and care.

- Compassion and respect for parents are core values in Islam, and this hadith encourages children to recognize the profound sacrifices their parents have made and to respond with utmost kindness and compassion.

5. Service to Parents as an Ongoing Responsibility:

- The hadith teaches that a single grand gesture cannot fulfill a child's duty toward their parents. Rather, serving and honoring parents is an ongoing and continuous responsibility, encompassing small daily acts of kindness and larger efforts to care for their well-being.

- It highlights that children should consistently strive to make their parents' lives comfortable, showing love and care for them in every aspect.

6. Reminder of Human Limitations:

- The Prophet's (peace and blessings be upon him) response also reminds us that no human effort can fully match a mother's love and sacrifice. It calls for humility and recognition of human limitations, encouraging children to constantly strive for improvement in serving their parents without assuming they have done enough.

Hadith 10: The Incomparable Debt to Fathers: A Child's Duty of Gratitude and Service

Narrated by Abu Huraira: "A child cannot repay his father unless he finds him as a slave and buys him and sets him free." (Sahih Muslim Book 32, Hadith 1510)

Key Lessons

1. **Incomparable Parental Sacrifice**: This hadith illustrates that a child can never fully repay their father for the sacrifices and contributions he has made throughout the child's life. The specific example of freeing a father from slavery signifies the enormity of the parental contribution.

2. **The Depth of Parental Rights**: The Prophet (peace be upon him) highlights that the only situation where a child could theoretically "repay" their father is an extreme case (freeing him from slavery), which is unlikely to occur. This metaphor underscores the immense weight of a parent's sacrifice and the child's lifelong obligation to honor them.

3. **Recognition of Fathers' Role**: While mothers have a special status, this hadith stresses that fathers, too, deserve immense respect and gratitude for their lifelong care, guidance, and provision for their children.

Key Lessons from Both Hadiths

1. **The Immense Rights of Parents**:

- Both hadiths highlight the incomparable sacrifices made by parents for their children, specifically focusing on the mother's experience of childbirth and the father's provision and care. These hadiths demonstrate that no matter what a child does, they cannot fully repay the rights and sacrifices of their parents.

- In the first hadith, even a grand act, like carrying one's mother over a long distance, does not equal the pain and effort of childbirth. Similarly, the second hadith indicates that the only way a child could come close to repaying their father is by freeing him from slavery, a rare and significant act.

2. **The Unrepayable Sacrifices of Mothers and Fathers**:
- The **physical and emotional sacrifices** of mothers during pregnancy,

childbirth, and nurturing are depicted as so immense that even extraordinary acts of devotion cannot fully repay them. The Prophet's (peace and blessings be upon him) response in the first hadith serves as a reminder of the profound and lifelong sacrifices mothers make.

- Fathers, too, play a critical role in the child's life by providing and caring for them. The second hadith highlights the unique role of fathers in protecting and providing for their children, emphasizing that their sacrifices are also unrepayable, except in extraordinary circumstances.

3. The Limitlessness of Parental Rights:

- Both hadiths emphasize the **limitlessness** of parents' rights over their children. These rights cannot be fully repaid through singular acts of kindness or lifelong service. Thus, children's responsibility to honor, serve, and respect their parents is continuous and unceasing throughout their lives.

- This teaches children that serving and honoring parents is a lifetime obligation and that they must strive to show kindness, care, and respect at every stage of their parents' lives.

4. Humility in Service to Parents:

- These hadiths remind children to approach their duties toward their parents with **humility**, recognizing that no matter what they do, they will never fully repay their parents' efforts. Carrying one's mother or providing for one's father should not be seen as enough to "repay" them but rather as part of a lifelong commitment.

- This lesson encourages children to continually serve and care for their parents without assuming they have fulfilled their obligations completely.

5. Parents as a Gateway to Paradise:

- In Islam, parents are regarded as one of the primary means of gaining Allah's pleasure and entering Paradise. These hadiths reinforce that serving and respecting parents is not only a moral obligation but also a spiritual one, and it is closely tied to a person's success in the Hereafter.

- Children can draw closer to Allah and earn His mercy and favor by constantly serving and seeking their parents' pleasure.

6. The Value of Sacrificial Acts Toward Parents:
- Although the Prophet (peace and blessings be upon him) emphasizes that no act can fully repay parents, both hadiths highlight the importance of sacrificial acts toward parents. Carrying a mother, providing for a father, or doing extraordinary acts for their well-being are still highly meritorious, even if they do not equal the parents' sacrifices.

- Children are encouraged to strive to do as much as possible to serve and care for their parents, even if they know they can never fully repay them.

7. Gratitude and Continuous Effort:
- These hadiths emphasize the importance of **gratitude** toward parents and recognition of their immense efforts. Children should strive to express gratitude through actions and words, acknowledging that their parents' sacrifices are immeasurable.

- The lesson is that children should never feel they have "done enough" for their parents. Instead, they should constantly seek ways to serve them.

8. The Unique Status of Mothers and Fathers:
- Both hadiths acknowledge the unique contributions of mothers and fathers. The focus on the mother's role in childbirth and nurturing in the first hadith and the focus on the father's role in provision and protection in the second hadith reflect the complementary yet equally important roles of both parents in a child's life.

- Islam emphasizes that honoring both parents is crucial, and each parent's contributions should be recognized and respected.

Conclusion

These hadiths highlight the immeasurable sacrifices made by parents and the **continuous** obligation of children to honor and serve them. No matter the extent of a child's service, it can never fully repay the rights of parents, especially the sacrifices made by mothers during childbirth and by fathers in providing for their children. Children are encouraged to maintain a deep sense of gratitude, humility, and commitment to serving their parents. These teachings reinforce the critical role of parents in a child's life and remind children that their duty to their parents is lifelong and essential to earning Allah's pleasure and success in the Hereafter.

Chapter 5

Honoring and Dutifulness to Parents Even After Their Death

Hadith 11: The Benefit of Charity on Behalf of a Deceased Parent: Saad ibn Ubadah's Gift for His Mother

Narrated by Abdullah ibn Abbas (may Allah be pleased with him): Saad ibn Ubadah (may Allah be pleased with him) asked the Prophet (peace and blessings be upon him): "O Messenger of Allah, my mother has died while I was away from her. Will it benefit her if I give charity on her behalf?" The Prophet (peace and blessings be upon him) said, "Yes." Saad said, "I bear witness that my two sheepfolds are charity for her." (Sahih al-Bukhari, Hadith 2760)

Key Lessons

1. **Charity on Behalf of the Deceased is Beneficial**: The hadith confirms that giving charity on behalf of a deceased person can benefit them in the Hereafter. This provides comfort and hope for those wishing to continue to benefit their loved ones after they have passed

away. It highlights Allah's mercy and generosity, who allows the deceased to receive rewards from the actions of the living even after their deeds have ceased.

2. **Continued Duty Toward Deceased Parents**: Children have the ability and responsibility to continue benefiting their parents even after death. This hadith demonstrates that honoring parents does not end when they pass away; it continues through acts of charity, prayers, and other righteous deeds performed in their name. It emphasizes the value of ongoing kindness and loyalty to parents, reinforcing the Islamic principle of lifelong respect and dutifulness toward them.

3. **Sadaqah Jariyah (Ongoing Charity)**: This hadith touches on the concept of **Sadaqah Jariyah**, or continuous charity, which continues to benefit the deceased for as long as the charitable act continues to benefit others. Examples include building wells, donating to causes that help people over time, or providing ongoing services to the community. The donation of Saad's sheepfolds is an example of this type of charity that can continuously provide for others and, therefore, benefit his mother long after her passing.

4. **The Prophet's Encouragement of Charity**: The Prophet's (peace and blessings be upon him) affirmative response encourages Muslims to give charity for the sake of their loved ones. This demonstrates Islam's emphasis on charity as one of the most virtuous deeds, especially when done with the sincere intention of benefiting others, including deceased family members. It reflects the Prophet's broader encouragement of charitable deeds and acts of generosity to earn rewards in this life and the Hereafter.

5. **Flexibility and Compassion in Islamic Teachings**: This hadith highlights the compassionate and flexible nature of Islamic teachings, which allow the living to contribute to the spiritual well-being of the deceased. It shows that Islam offers multiple ways to benefit those who have passed, including charity, supplication, and fulfilling their vows.

6. **Moral Responsibility for Loved Ones**: Saad's concern for his mother's well-being, even after her death, reflects children's deep moral responsibility toward their parents. This hadith reinforces the value of maintaining this responsibility through righteous actions to benefit the deceased in the Afterlife.

Hadith 12: Three Ongoing Sources of Reward After Death: Charity, Knowledge, and Righteous Offspring

Narrated by Abu Hurairah (may Allah be pleased with him): The Prophet (peace and blessings be upon him) said: "When a person dies, his deeds are cut off except for three: ongoing charity, beneficial knowledge, or a righteous child who prays for him." (Sahih Muslim, Book 13, Hadith 4005)

Key Lessons

1. **Deeds that continue after death**:
   While most deeds cease upon death, three specific actions continue to benefit a person in the afterlife:

   - **Ongoing charity (sadaqah jariyah)**: Charitable acts whose benefits endure, such as building wells, schools, or mosques.

   - **Beneficial knowledge**: Teaching or sharing knowledge that continues to benefit others, such as writing books or educating others in faith, morality, or skill.

   - **A righteous child who prays for them**: A pious child who prays for the deceased parents is considered a source of ongoing benefit, highlighting the importance of raising children with strong moral and spiritual values.

Hadith 13: Fulfilling Vows for Deceased Parents: A Daughter's Duty to Complete Her Mother's Fast

Narrated by Abdullah ibn Abbas (may Allah be pleased with him): A woman came to the Prophet (peace and blessings be upon him) and said, "My mother has passed away, but she had a vow to fast. Shall I fulfill her vow?" The Prophet said, "Yes, fulfill it on her behalf." (Sahih al-Bukhari, Hadith 1953)

Key Lessons

1. **Fulfilling Vows on Behalf of the Deceased**: This hadith shows that a living person can fulfill the religious obligations or vows of a deceased relative, such as fasting. The Prophet (peace be upon him) allowed the daughter to complete her mother's vow, indicating that such acts of devotion can still be completed after death by others on their behalf. It highlights that responsibilities and religious commitments, especially vows made to Allah, are to be taken seriously, even if the person passes away before completing them.

2. **The Continuation of Good Deeds**: This hadith illustrates that family members can contribute to the spiritual benefit of their deceased loved ones. By fulfilling the mother's vow, the daughter ensured that her mother's commitment to Allah was honored, and the reward for the fast could be counted toward her mother in the Hereafter. It reflects the continuity of familial responsibility, where living relatives can complete unfinished good deeds, ensuring that the spiritual benefits are not lost.

3. **The Concept of Niyyah (Intention)**: Fulfilling a vow on behalf of someone else is closely related to the concept of **niyyah** (intention). The daughter's intention, in this case, was to fulfill her mother's promise to Allah. This hadith teaches that sincere intentions and actions done for the benefit of another can be rewarded by Allah, even if the original vow-maker has passed away. It also emphasizes the importance of making good intentions and following through on them in one's lifetime,

knowing that others may help fulfill them after death if necessary.

4. **Respecting the Wishes of Deceased Relatives**: The Prophet's (peace be upon him) response shows that respecting the wishes of deceased loved ones, particularly their religious vows, is important in Islam. This hadith encourages family members to honor the commitments made by the deceased, ensuring that they receive the reward for those actions. It is a reminder that even after a person has passed away, their spiritual journey continues, and those who remain can help them by fulfilling the obligations they intended to complete.

5. **Islam's Flexibility in Fulfilling Religious Duties**: This hadith demonstrates the flexibility and mercy within Islamic law, allowing for fulfilling religious obligations by proxy when someone can no longer do so. It highlights that in cases where individuals cannot complete acts of worship, Islam provides solutions that allow others to step in and fulfill those duties. The hadith also indicates that such acts are not restricted to fasting but can extend to other religious obligations or vows, such as prayers, Hajj, or charity.

6. **Importance of Vows (Nadhr) in Islam**: The hadith shows the seriousness of *nadhr* (vows) in Islam. A vow made to Allah is a commitment that should not be taken lightly. Even after the person's death, the unfulfilled vow remains, and their heirs or relatives must fulfill it if possible. The obligation to fulfill vows is considered a sign of faithfulness and loyalty to one's commitment to Allah, reflecting one's integrity and dedication to fulfilling religious duties.

Hadith 14: Honoring Parents After Death: Acts of Righteousness to Benefit Deceased Parents

Narrated by Abu Usayd Malik ibn Rabi'ah: "A man asked the Prophet (peace and blessings be upon him): 'Is there anything I can do for my parents after they have passed away?' The Prophet (peace and blessings be upon him) replied: 'Yes, you can pray for them, seek forgiveness for them, fulfill their promises, and maintain ties with their relatives.'" (Sunan Abu Dawood, Book 42, Hadith 5123)

Key Lessons

1. **Continuing good deeds for deceased parents**:
   Even after the passing of one's parents, a child can still benefit them by engaging in acts that reflect their honor and uphold their legacy.

2. **Actions that benefit deceased parents**:

- **Praying for them**: Making supplications (du'a) for the well-being of their souls in the hereafter.

- **Seeking forgiveness for them**: Asking Allah to forgive their sins.

- **Fulfilling their promises**: Carrying out any unfulfilled commitments or obligations they may have left behind.

- **Maintaining ties with their relatives**: Keeping good relations with family members connected to one's parents reflects respect and gratitude toward the parents.

The hadiths collectively emphasize that a child's duties to their parents do not end with their passing. Islam encourages believers to continue honoring their parents even after their death through righteous deeds such as charity, fulfilling their vows, making du'a (supplications), seeking forgiveness for them, and maintaining ties with their relatives. These acts ensure that the deceased continue to receive rewards, even though their personal deeds have ceased.

One of the key principles derived from these hadiths is the concept of *Sadaqah Jariyah* (ongoing charity), which continues to benefit both the living and the dead. Whether it is giving charity on behalf of deceased parents, fulfilling vows they were unable to complete, or engaging in acts of worship like prayer and supplication for their forgiveness, Islam offers various ways for children to continue serving their parents beyond the grave.

Furthermore, these hadiths reflect the mercy and flexibility of Islamic teachings, allowing for unfulfilled obligations or desires of the deceased to be completed by their living relatives. This reinforces the idea that family bonds hold immense significance in this world and the Hereafter, especially between parents and children.

These teachings highlight the importance of maintaining a deep sense of responsibility and respect toward parents, encouraging continuous acts of devotion, kindness, and remembrance, even after their death. This ongoing care reflects the enduring nature of family ties in Islam and ensures that the deceased continues to benefit from the righteous deeds of their loved ones.

Chapter 6

Respecting Parents Even if They Are Non-Muslim

Hadith 15: Maintaining Ties with Non-Muslim Parents: The Prophet's Guidance to Asma bint Abu Bakr

Narrated by Asma bint Abu Bakr (may Allah be pleased with her): My mother, who was still an idolater, came to visit me at the time of the Messenger of Allah (peace and blessings be upon him). I asked the Prophet (peace and blessings be upon him), "My mother has come to me and she is asking for my help; should I maintain ties with her?" He said, "Yes, maintain ties with your mother." (Sahih al-Bukhari, Hadith 2620)

Key Lesson

- Islam teaches maintaining strong ties with one's parents, regardless of their religious beliefs. The duty to honor and serve parents is not limited to Muslim parents.

Hadith 16: Kindness to Non-Muslim Parents: The Prophet's Command to Honor Mothers

Narrated by Abdullah ibn Amr (may Allah be pleased with him): The Prophet (peace and blessings be upon him) said: "Be good to your mother," even if she was not a Muslim. (Al-Adab Al-Mufrad, Hadith 8)

Key Lesson

- A child's duty to respect and serve their parents remains regardless of the parent's religious beliefs. This emphasizes the universal importance of parents' rights in Islam.

Key Lessons from Both Hadiths

1. **Maintaining Ties with Parents, Regardless of Their Faith**:

- Both hadiths emphasize the importance of maintaining strong family ties with one's parents, even if they are not Muslims. Islam teaches that honoring and being kind to one's parents is a fundamental duty that transcends religious differences.

- In the hadith of Asma bint Abu Bakr, despite her mother being an idolater, the Prophet (peace and blessings be upon him) affirmed the obligation to maintain ties with her. This demonstrates that Islam values family bonds, regardless of differing beliefs.

2. **Kindness to Mothers as a Core Islamic Duty**:

- The hadith of Abdullah ibn Amr stresses that one should be good to one's mother, even if she is not Muslim. Mothers, in particular, are given a special status in Islam, and being kind and dutiful to them is considered one of the most virtuous deeds.

- This hadith reinforces the high status of mothers in Islam, showing that their rights over their children remain intact, regardless of religious differences.

3. Islam Promotes Universal Morality:
- These hadiths highlight that **kindness, compassion, and maintaining good relationships** are core Islamic values that apply universally, regardless of faith or background. A Muslim's moral obligation to care for and maintain ties with their parents is not negated by religious differences.

- This demonstrates that Islam promotes mercy, tolerance, and good conduct in family and societal relations, fostering peaceful coexistence and mutual respect between people of different beliefs.

4. Balance Between Faith and Family Obligations:
- Islam encourages maintaining a balance between one's religious obligations and family responsibilities. While maintaining faith in Allah is paramount, Islam also teaches that fulfilling family obligations, particularly toward parents, is essential—even if parents are non-Muslims.

- This principle is evident in the Prophet's (peace be upon him) response to Asma bint Abu Bakr, who was unsure whether she should continue her relationship with her non-Muslim mother. The Prophet's clear instruction to maintain ties shows that family relationships should be preserved, even when faith differences exist.

5. The Prophetic Model of Mercy and Compassion:
- The Prophet Muhammad (peace and blessings be upon him) consistently modeled mercy and compassion in his teachings, as reflected in these hadiths. His guidance to Asma and Abdullah ibn Amr demonstrates the importance of treating non-Muslim parents with respect, love, and care.

- This illustrates the inclusive and compassionate nature of Islam, where familial bonds are upheld as sacred, regardless of religious belief.

6. Maintaining Ties is a Form of Dawah (Invitation to Islam):
- By maintaining good relations with non-Muslim parents, Muslims can exemplify the beauty of Islamic values. Treating parents with kindness and respect may serve as a form of *dawah* (invitation to Islam) by showing the universality of Islamic morality and its emphasis on family values.

- Maintaining positive relations with non-Muslim family members can leave a lasting impression and foster understanding between people of different faiths.

7. Kindness to Parents is a Lifelong Obligation:
- Both hadiths stress that the obligation to be kind and dutiful to one's parents is lifelong, and it does not end with differences in religious belief. Whether a parent is Muslim or not, the child remains responsible for treating them well and maintaining a relationship of respect and care.

- This teaches Muslims that family obligations remain a priority, regardless of personal differences or religious disagreements.

8. Setting Boundaries While Maintaining Ties:
- While Islam emphasizes maintaining ties and showing kindness to non-Muslim parents, it also sets boundaries when it comes to matters of faith. Muslims must prioritize their obedience to Allah, but this does not mean severing ties or mistreating parents who hold different beliefs.

- The hadiths encourage Muslims to navigate these relationships with care, ensuring that respect for parents is maintained without compromising their own religious principles.

Conclusion

These hadiths emphasize the fundamental importance of maintaining family ties and being kind to one's parents, even if they do not share the same faith. Islam upholds the sanctity of family relationships and encourages Muslims to honor and care for their parents regardless of religious differences. The teachings of the Prophet Muhammad (peace be upon him) demonstrate that kindness and respect toward parents is a universal obligation in Islam, reflecting the values of mercy, compassion, and tolerance. These hadiths serve as a reminder that family bonds should be preserved and that being good to one's parents is a cornerstone of Islamic ethics.

Chapter 7

Protecting Parental Honor

Hadith 17: The Grave Sin of Cursing One's Parents Through Indirect Abuse

Narrated by Abdullah ibn Amr: One of the greatest sins is for a man to curse his parents." The people asked, 'O Messenger of Allah, how does a man curse his parents?' He said, 'He abuses the father of another man, and that man abuses his father in return, and he abuses his mother, and that man abuses his mother in return.'" (Sahih al-Bukhari, Book 78, Hadith 4)

Key Lessons

1. **Indirect Disrespect Toward Parents is a Grave Sin**:

- This hadith highlights that disrespect toward parents does not always happen directly. By engaging in abusive or inappropriate behavior toward others, one can indirectly cause harm or disrespect to their parents. The Prophet (peace be upon him) warns against this behavior, as it is considered one of the major sins in Islam.

- It teaches that one's actions have consequences that can affect the dignity and honor of one's parents.

2. The Seriousness of Parental Honor in Islam:

- Islam places immense importance on honoring and respecting one's parents. This hadith shows that disrespecting parents, even indirectly, is regarded as one of the greatest sins. Respecting parents is not only about personal behavior toward them but also about how one conducts oneself with others.

- The hadith underscores the severity of parental respect by linking it to divine punishment for those who fail to protect their parents' honor.

3. Avoiding Harmful and Abusive Speech:

- The hadith highlights the ripple effect of abusive speech. Insulting others leads to discord and can escalate into more serious consequences, such as involving one's parents in the exchange of insults. This reinforces the Islamic principle of guarding one's tongue and avoiding harmful speech toward others.

- It teaches that cursing and abusive language can have far-reaching consequences that affect individuals and their families, including their parents.

4. Personal Responsibility for One's Actions:

- A key lesson from this hadith is the concept of **personal responsibility**. One must be conscious of one's behavior toward others, as it can lead to unintended harm to one's parents. The hadith teaches Muslims to be mindful of how their actions can lead to situations that dishonor their parents, even if indirectly.

- This highlights the interconnectedness of human relationships and the responsibility to maintain the dignity of one's family through righteous behavior.

5. Preventing Retaliation and Negative Cycles:

- The hadith demonstrates how negative behavior, such as cursing or abusing others, often leads to retaliation, creating a cycle of animosity that can extend to one's family. One can prevent such cycles by behaving respectfully and avoiding abusive language.

- It teaches the importance of self-control and maintaining a high standard of conduct to avoid harm, especially toward one's family.

6. **Broad Understanding of Parental Rights**:
   - The hadith expands the understanding of parental rights beyond direct interaction. One is responsible for protecting their parents' dignity and honor in all aspects of life, including in their dealings with others. It teaches that protecting the reputation and respect of one's parents is part of being dutiful to them.

   - The emphasis on avoiding situations that could lead to parents being cursed demonstrates the broader responsibility children have toward safeguarding their parents' honor.

Conclusion:

This hadith teaches that respecting parents goes beyond direct interactions and includes avoiding behaviors that could lead to indirect dishonor, such as engaging in abusive speech toward others. It highlights the seriousness of safeguarding parental honor. It teaches Muslims to be mindful of their actions and words, as they can have far-reaching consequences that impact not only themselves but their families. Respecting parents is an essential part of Islamic ethics, and this hadith serves as a powerful reminder to avoid any behavior that could lead to their dishonor, even indirectly.

Chapter 8

Being Kind and Gentle to Parents

Hadith 18: The Duty of Humility and Mercy Toward Parents: A Qur'anic Command (Quran 17:24)

"Lower unto them the wing of humility out of mercy, and say: My Lord, have mercy upon them as they raised me when I was small." (Quran 17:24 - Tafsir Hadith explanation by Ibn Kathir)

Key Lessons

1. **Humility and Compassion Toward Parents**: The verse teaches the importance of lowering oneself in humility before parents as a sign of respect and compassion. This humility comes from a place of mercy and gratitude for the care parents provided during childhood.

2. **Praying for Parents**: It emphasizes the significance of continually praying for parents, asking Allah to show mercy upon them just as they were merciful and nurturing during one's upbringing. This highlights the ongoing duty to honor parents, even through prayer, long after one

has grown up.

3. **Mercy and Reciprocity**: The verse reflects the principle of reciprocating the care parents provide. Just as parents raise their children with love and sacrifice, children should return this kindness with mercy and humility toward them, particularly in their old age.

Hadith 19: The Greatest of Major Sins: Shirk and Disobedience to Parents

Narrated by Abu Bakrah: The Messenger of Allah (peace and blessings be upon him) said: "Shall I not inform you of the greatest of the major sins?" They said, "Yes, O Messenger of Allah." He said, "Associating others with Allah (shirk) and being undutiful to one's parents." (Sahih al-Bukhari, Book 78, Hadith 3; Sahih Muslim, Book 1, Hadith 161)

Key Lessons

1. **Shirk (Associating Partners with Allah) as the Gravest Sin**: This hadith identifies the most serious sin in Islam—associating others with Allah (shirk), which is considered a violation of the fundamental belief in monotheism (Tawhid).

2. **Disobedience to Parents as a Major Sin**: Alongside shirk, the Prophet (peace be upon him) emphasizes being undutiful or disobedient to one's parents as one of the greatest sins. This reflects the high status parents hold in Islam and the severity of neglecting or mistreating them.

3. **The Link Between Worship and Filial Duty**: The pairing of shirk with disobedience to parents in this hadith underscores the close connection between a person's relationship with Allah and their treatment of parents. Just as shirk disrupts one's relationship with the Creator, being undutiful to parents severely damages one's moral and

spiritual standing.

Common Themes:

- **Parental Respect and Honor**: The Quranic verse and the hadith emphasize the importance of respecting, honoring, and serving one's parents with humility and compassion. The value of showing mercy to parents mirrors the mercy they showed during the child's upbringing.

- **Spiritual Consequences of Disrespect**: The hadith highlights that neglecting or mistreating parents is a grave sin, comparable to shirk, indicating the severe consequences of being undutiful to parents in Islam.

- **Continued Care and Prayer for Parents**: Both texts stress the significance of caring for parents not only physically and emotionally but also spiritually by making supplications for their well-being and mercy from Allah. This teaches that filial duty also extends beyond mere actions into the spiritual realm.

Key Takeaways:

- Filial piety in Islam is deeply connected to one's relationship with Allah, and neglecting parents is seen as a serious offense with major spiritual consequences.

- Humility, compassion, and ongoing prayer are vital ways to show respect and honor to one's parents, whether alive or deceased.

In conclusion, the Quranic verse and the hadith emphasize the paramount importance of honoring and respecting one's parents in Islam. The verse from the Quran calls for humility, mercy, and continual supplication for parents, reflecting the care and love they provided during childhood. The hadith pairs disobedience to parents with shirk (associating partners with Allah), indicating that neglecting or mistreating one's parents is one of the gravest sins in Islam. Together, these teachings underscore that respecting parents is a social obligation and a profound spiritual duty directly linked to one's relationship with Allah. Filial piety, marked by humility, compassion, and prayer, is central to living a righteous and morally sound life in Islam.

Chapter 9

The Importance of Patience and Forbearance with Parents

Hadith 20: The Path to Paradise: Fulfilling the Rights of Allah and Parents

Narrated by Ibn Abbas (may Allah be pleased with him): The Prophet (peace and blessings be upon him) said: "Whoever wakes up in the morning having fulfilled the rights of Allah and the rights of his parents, then Allah will open two gates of Paradise for him. And if he wakes up displeasing Allah but pleasing his parents, then Allah will open one gate of Paradise for him. And if his parents are displeased with him, Allah will not be pleased with him until his parents are pleased with him." (Al-Adab Al-Mufrad, Hadith 5)

Key Lessons

1. **Fulfilling Both Divine and Parental Rights**:
   - This hadith emphasizes the importance of balancing two major

responsibilities in Islam: fulfilling the rights of Allah (through worship and devotion) and fulfilling the rights of one's parents (through respect, care, and obedience). Both are essential for a believer's success in this world and the Hereafter.

- Attaining Allah's pleasure and earning Paradise requires not only piety and devotion but also dutifulness toward one's parents.

2. The High Status of Parents in Islam:

- Pleasing one's parents is directly linked to earning Allah's pleasure, which highlights the exalted status of parents in Islam. This hadith teaches that children should prioritize honoring, respecting, and serving their parents as a key to securing Allah's blessings.

- The fact that Allah will not be pleased with someone until their parents are pleased underscores the seriousness of maintaining good relations with one's parents.

3. Two Gates of Paradise:

- The promise of **two gates of Paradise** opening for someone who fulfills both Allah's and their parents' rights symbolizes the abundant reward awaiting those who maintain a balanced, righteous life in their spiritual and familial duties.

- Even if someone displeases Allah but manages to please their parents, one gate of Paradise will still be opened for them, showing the immense weight of parental respect in Islam.

4. Displeasing Parents Brings Allah's Displeasure:

- If someone angers or neglects their parents, Allah's displeasure is directly linked to this behavior, regardless of other acts of worship. This hadith teaches that parental respect is non-negotiable and that maintaining good relations with one's parents is crucial for gaining Allah's favor.

Hadith 21: Parental Rights Over Wealth: 'You and Your Wealth Belong to Your Father

Narrated by Abdullah ibn Amr (may Allah be pleased with him): The Prophet (peace and blessings be upon him) said: "A man came to the Prophet (peace and blessings be upon him) and said, 'O Messenger of Allah, I have wealth and children, and my father needs my wealth.' The Prophet (peace and blessings be upon him) said, 'You and your wealth belong to your father.'" (Sunan Ibn Majah, Hadith 2291)

Key Lessons

1. **Parents' Rights Over Their Children's Wealth**:

- This hadith highlights the rights of parents over their children's wealth. A father (or parent) has the right to benefit from their child's wealth, especially when in need. This teaches that children are responsible for supporting their parents financially if required, just as parents took care of their children when they were young.

- The phrase "you and your wealth belong to your father" shows the extent of a child's duty to their parents, especially in providing for their needs.

2. **Emphasis on Parental Support and Responsibility**:
- Islam places great emphasis on fulfilling the needs of parents, especially as they age or face financial hardship. Children are encouraged to be generous and responsible toward their parents, ensuring their well-being without hesitation.

- The hadith teaches that financially supporting one's parents is not an obligation to be viewed as burdensome but an honor and duty.

3. **Respecting Parental Authority and Needs**:
- The Prophet's (peace and blessings be upon him) response reflects the

respect and deference children must show toward their parents. Even in matters of wealth, children are reminded that their resources are not entirely their own but should be shared with their parents when necessary.

- It teaches the Islamic principle of gratitude toward parents by ensuring their needs are met as part of dutifulness and respect.

4. **Balance Between Rights and Responsibilities**:
   - While parents have a right to their children's wealth, this hadith also teaches that such rights must be exercised with wisdom and fairness. Parental needs should be met, but this responsibility should not be abused. The goal is to maintain a balance where both the parent's needs are fulfilled and the child's wealth is used responsibly.

Lessons from Both Hadiths

1. **Fulfilling Parental Rights is Central to Gaining Allah's Pleasure**:

- Both hadiths emphasize the immense importance of fulfilling the rights of one's parents. In the first hadith, respecting and serving parents is directly tied to attaining Allah's pleasure and entering Paradise. In the second hadith, supporting one's parents financially is viewed as part of the children's duty to care for their parents, reinforcing the respect and honor due to them.

2. **The Interconnection of Divine and Parental Rights**:
   - These hadiths teach that fulfilling the rights of Allah and fulfilling the rights of parents are closely linked. A person who maintains good relations with their parents and ensures their well-being will find divine blessings while neglecting or angering one's parents can result in Allah's displeasure.

3. Parental Authority and the Child's Duty:

- Both hadiths highlight parents' high level of respect and authority over their children in Islam. Children are expected to prioritize their parents' well-being, whether it be through emotional, physical, or financial support.

4. Holistic Responsibility in Islam:

- These hadiths demonstrate that Islam calls for a holistic sense of responsibility, where one must balance spiritual devotion (fulfilling Allah's rights) and social obligations (fulfilling the rights of parents). This balance is key to achieving success in both this world and the Hereafter.

These hadiths reinforce the deep connection between honoring one's parents and earning Allah's favor, teaching Muslims that serving and supporting parents is not only a moral duty but a pathway to spiritual success and ultimate salvation.

BOOK REVIEW REQUEST

Dear Reader,

Thank you for **exploring "Keys to Paradise: Serving Parents with Excellence: Forty Hadiths on Honoring and Respecting Parents."** Your support and engagement mean so much to me. I hope the book has enriched your understanding and offered practical guidance for your personal and spiritual growth.

I would be deeply grateful if you could take a moment to share your thoughts on the book. Reviews play an essential role in helping others discover valuable insights, and your feedback can truly make a difference. Whether you post your review on Amazon, Goodreads, or any other platform, your honest reflections are greatly appreciated and will help spread this important message to a broader audience.

https://www.amazon.com/review/review-your-purchases/?asin=B0DKBRQ54W

With sincere gratitude,
Aisha Othman

Chapter 10

Honoring Parents in Their Old Age

Hadith 22: The Disgrace of Neglecting Elderly Parents: A Missed Opportunity for Paradise

Narrated by Abu Huraira: The Prophet (Allah bless him and grant him peace) said, "May he be disgraced! May he be disgraced! May he be disgraced!" They asked, "Who, O Messenger of Allah?" He said, "The one whose parents, one or both of them, reach old age during his lifetime but he does not enter Paradise by serving them." (Sahih Muslim, Book 45, Hadith 6189)

Key Lessons

1. **Opportunity for Paradise Through Serving Parents**: This hadith emphasizes the immense opportunity and blessing of serving one's parents, especially when they reach old age. Caring for elderly parents is portrayed as a direct path to attaining Paradise, highlighting the spiritual rewards associated with filial piety.

2. **Grave Consequences of Neglecting Parents**: The repetition of "May

he be disgraced!" emphasizes the seriousness of failing to care for one's parents in their old age. Neglecting this duty is considered a grave shortcoming in Islam, resulting in the loss of a major opportunity for salvation and divine reward.

3. **Parents as a Test in Old Age**: The hadith indicates that Allah provides children with a unique opportunity to earn His pleasure by serving their parents when they are elderly and dependent. It reflects the Islamic belief that honoring parents is a duty and a way to seek closeness to Allah.

Hadith 23: The Reward of Caring for Elderly Parents: Under Allah's Shade on the Day of Judgment

"The one who looks after and provides for his parents at their old age, while they are dependent on him, will be under the Shade of Allah's Throne on the Day of Judgment." (Al-Hakim in his collection Al-Mustadrak)

Key Lessons

1. **Special Status for Those Who Care for Elderly Parents**: This hadith highlights the high spiritual status granted to those who care for their parents in old age. Being under the Shade of Allah's Throne on the Day of Judgment is a significant reward reserved for those who perform exemplary acts of worship and kindness.

2. **Protection and Mercy on the Day of Judgment**: Being under Allah's Shade symbolizes protection from the hardships of the Day of Judgment. This illustrates that serving and caring for one's parents in their time of need is rewarded in this life and provides immense spiritual protection in the hereafter.

3. **Elderly Parents as a Source of Blessing**: The hadith reflects that elderly parents are a source of immense blessing and opportunity

for children. Caring for them provides a path to divine mercy and rewards on the Day of Judgment, encouraging children to embrace this responsibility with gratitude.

Common Themes:

- **Serving Elderly Parents as a Path to Paradise**: Both hadiths emphasize that caring for one's parents in their old age is a key to earning Allah's pleasure and entering Paradise. This duty is portrayed as one of the highest forms of worship and service.

- **Consequences of Neglecting Parents**: The first hadith warns of the spiritual disgrace and loss for those who fail to serve their parents during their lifetime, while the second hadith promises immense rewards for those who fulfill this responsibility.

- **Divine Protection for Caregivers of Parents**: The second hadith emphasizes that those who serve their elderly parents will receive divine protection and mercy on the Day of Judgment, indicating the far-reaching spiritual benefits of this act of kindness.

Key Takeaways:

- Caring for elderly parents is a profound duty and an incredible opportunity to earn Paradise and divine favor. Failing to fulfill this responsibility results in spiritual loss, but while fulfilling it brings blessings in this life and the hereafter.

- The hadiths stress that parents, especially in their old age, offer their children the chance to demonstrate compassion, patience, and devotion. Allah highly rewards these acts, both in terms of entry into Paradise and protection on the Day of Judgment.

- Serving one's parents is a societal obligation and a significant spiritual act with long-lasting rewards.

In conclusion, both hadiths emphasize the immense spiritual significance of caring for one's parents, particularly when they reach old age. Serving and providing for elderly parents is seen as a direct path to earning Allah's pleasure and attaining Paradise while neglecting this responsibility results in serious spiritual consequences. The hadiths highlight that caring for parents is not just a moral obligation but a unique opportunity to receive divine mercy and protection, especially on the Day of Judgment. Through these teachings, Islam underscores the importance of filial piety and the blessings from fulfilling the duty of honoring and caring for one's parents in their time of need.

Chapter 11

Respect for Parent's Wishes

Hadith 24: The Pleasure of Allah Lies in Parental Obedience: A Call to Sacrifice for Parents' Satisfaction

Narrated by Abdullah ibn 'Umar: "The pleasure of the Lord is in the pleasure of the parent, and the displeasure of the Lord is in the displeasure of the parent. Even if your parents ask you to leave your family and wealth, leave them and obey them." (Sahih Ibn Hibban, Hadith 429)

Key Lessons

1. **Divine Pleasure Linked to Parental Satisfaction**: This hadith highlights the profound connection between pleasing one's parents and earning the pleasure of Allah. The happiness or displeasure of one's parents directly affects one's relationship with Allah.

2. **Obedience to Parents**: The hadith emphasizes that obeying parents is a fundamental obligation in Islam, even to the extent of sacrificing personal wealth or comfort. This teaches that the rights and respect owed to parents take precedence over material possessions or personal desires.

3. **Parental Authority**: It stresses that obedience to parents should be a priority, signaling that pleasing them is not merely a social expectation but a spiritual obligation with significant consequences.

Hadith 25: Parental Authority and Personal Choices: The Duty of Obeying Parents in Marital Decisions

Narrated by Abdullah ibn Umar (may Allah be pleased with him): I had a wife whom I loved, but my father disliked her. My father ordered me to divorce her, but I refused. I mentioned this to the Prophet (peace and blessings be upon him), and he said, "O Abdullah ibn Umar, obey your father." (Sunan Abu Dawood, Hadith 5138)

Key Lessons

1. **Obedience to Parents**:

- This hadith underscores the importance of **obedience to parents**, even in matters of personal choice, such as marriage. The Prophet (peace and blessings be upon him) instructed Abdullah ibn Umar to follow his father's command, highlighting that children should take their parents' wishes seriously and honor them, particularly when the advice comes from someone wise and righteous, like Umar ibn al-Khattab.

- Obedience to parents is a central tenet in Islam, and this hadith reinforces the value of respecting their opinions, especially when it comes to major life decisions.

2. **Parental Guidance in Personal Matters**:
- The hadith teaches that parents often have greater life experience and insight, which can lead to wise decisions regarding their children's personal lives. Although Abdullah ibn Umar loved his wife, his father's advice was rooted in a broader understanding of the situation.

- Children should value and consider parents' guidance in such personal matters, particularly when based on wisdom, sincerity, and care, even when the decisions are emotionally difficult.

3. Balancing Love and Obedience:
- This hadith reflects the emotional conflict that can arise between personal desires and the duty of obedience to parents. Abdullah ibn Umar loved his wife but was instructed by the Prophet (peace and blessings be upon him) to prioritize obedience to his father. This demonstrates the delicate balance between following one's emotions and fulfilling religious obligations toward one's parents.

- It emphasizes that obedience to parents, when their advice is reasonable and aligned with Islamic principles, may sometimes take precedence over personal preferences, particularly in situations that have long-term consequences.

4. Consultation with the Prophet (peace and blessings be upon him):
- Abdullah ibn Umar's decision to consult the Prophet (peace and blessings be upon him) before making his final decision shows the importance of seeking wise counsel when faced with difficult situations. The Prophet's (peace and blessings be upon him) judgment provided clarity and reinforced the Islamic principle of respecting parental authority.

- This highlights the value of seeking guidance from knowledgeable and trusted sources in situations that require careful deliberation, especially when dealing with sensitive personal matters.

5. Parental Authority and Islamic Ethics:
- The hadith teaches that parents have a significant role in guiding their children, even in marital decisions. However, the advice or command of the parents should be rooted in **Islamic ethics**, fairness, and genuine concern for the well-being of their child. Umar ibn al-Khattab, being a righteous man, was acting out of wisdom and concern for his

son's welfare, and the Prophet's (peace and blessings be upon him) instruction to obey him reflects this context.

- It also suggests that obedience to parents is not absolute if their demands contradict Islamic principles or are unjust. However, in this case, the Prophet's (peace and blessings be upon him) approval of Umar's decision shows the father's guidance was valid and aligned with Islamic values.

6. **The Role of Fathers in Decision-Making**:
    - This hadith illustrates the prominent role of fathers in guiding their children, particularly in crucial decisions like marriage. Umar ibn al-Khattab, known for his wisdom and piety, provided direction to his son based on his understanding of what would benefit him in the long term.

    - It also points to fathers' responsibility to ensure that their decisions and advice are made in the best interests of their children and are in accordance with Islamic principles.

7. **The Importance of Maintaining Family Harmony**:
    - Although it may seem harsh to be asked to divorce a loved one, the hadith shows that family harmony and the importance of parental approval can sometimes take precedence. Abdullah ibn Umar was asked to prioritize maintaining a respectful and obedient relationship with his father, which in turn preserves the overall harmony of the family unit.

    - This hadith highlights that decisions should not be made solely based on personal feelings but with consideration for the broader family context and the preservation of respect and unity.

Key Lessons from the Hadiths

1. **Obedience to Parents is Paramount:** Both hadiths emphasize the

critical importance of obeying one's parents, even when it involves personal sacrifices such as wealth, family, or relationships. In the first hadith, the Prophet Muhammad (peace and blessings be upon him) highlights that pleasing parents leads to the pleasure of Allah, and displeasing them leads to His displeasure. This underscores the weight Islam places on parental obedience as a pathway to spiritual success and divine satisfaction.

2. **Divine Connection Through Parental Pleasure**: The first hadith teaches that a direct connection exists between pleasing one's parents and pleasing Allah. Disobedience to parents, unless it involves sinful behavior, can distance one from Allah's mercy and pleasure. This connection reinforces that serving and honoring one's parents is a social obligation and a spiritual one that draws a person closer to Allah.

3. **Sacrifice for Parental Contentment**: Both hadiths discuss sacrifice for parental satisfaction. Whether it involves giving up material wealth or a beloved spouse, the hadiths demonstrate that parental guidance, when in accordance with Islamic principles, takes precedence over personal desires. Abdullah ibn Umar's example illustrates the extent to which obedience to parents should be taken, even in emotionally difficult circumstances.

4. **Prioritizing Parental Wishes Over Personal Desires**: The second hadith, in which Abdullah ibn Umar is advised by the Prophet (peace and blessings be upon him) to obey his father's request to divorce his wife, teaches a significant lesson: sometimes, personal desires must be subordinated for the sake of parental approval, even in sensitive matters like marriage. This hadith reflects the high status of parents and their ability to influence major decisions in their children's lives when it is within the bounds of Sharia.

5. **Balancing Parental Rights and Personal Well-being**: While the hadiths emphasize obeying parents, scholars stress that this obedience should not lead to injustice or harm. If a parent commands something

that goes against Islamic principles or causes undue harm, then the child is not obligated to obey. In the case of Abdullah ibn Umar, it is assumed that the father's disapproval had a valid reason that aligned with Islamic values, not merely personal preference.

Conclusion

These hadiths reflect parents' significant role in shaping their children's life and spiritual well-being in Islam. Pleasing and obeying parents, especially in matters permissible by Sharia, directly ties into one's relationship with Allah. The lessons derived from these hadiths highlight that honoring and serving parents is a pathway to earning Allah's pleasure and gaining divine blessings in this world and the Hereafter. However, while obedience to parents is stressed, it is balanced by Islamic guidelines that ensure fairness and protection of personal well-being, as obedience is not required in matters leading to sin or injustice.

Chapter 12

Supplicating for Parents

Hadith 26: The Elevation of a Parent's Status in Paradise Through a Child's Prayers

Narrated by Abu Huraira: The Prophet (peace and blessings be upon him) said: "Verily, Allah raises the status of a servant in Paradise, and he will say: 'O my Lord, how did I earn this?' Allah will say: 'By your child's seeking forgiveness for you.'" (Sunan Ibn Majah, Hadith 3660)

Key Lessons

1. **The Power of Du'a for Deceased Parents**:

- This hadith highlights the tremendous value of a child's du'a (supplication) and seeking forgiveness for their deceased parents. It shows that a child's prayers can have a direct and positive impact on their parents' status in the Hereafter, even after the parents' personal deeds have ceased.

- Children are encouraged to continuously seek forgiveness on behalf of their parents, knowing that this act can lead to the spiritual elevation of their parents.

2. Ongoing Rewards for the Deceased:
- The hadith reflects that a parent's deeds are not completely cut off after death. Children can continue to earn rewards for their parents by praying for them and seeking forgiveness, demonstrating that the spiritual connection between parents and children continues after death.

- It reinforces the idea of **Sadaqah Jariyah** (ongoing charity), where righteous actions performed by children benefit their parents, even after their passing.

3. The Mercy of Allah:
- The hadith shows Allah's boundless mercy and generosity. Despite the deceased being unable to perform any more deeds themselves, Allah still allows them to benefit from the righteous acts of their children, which can elevate their rank in Paradise.

- It teaches that Allah's mercy encompasses the good deeds of others, particularly those of a person's family members, offering hope and blessings for the deceased.

4. Children's Responsibility to Honor Their Parents:
- This hadith highlights the ongoing responsibility of children to honor their parents even after their death. Children can continue to show dutifulness by praying for their parents, seeking forgiveness for them, and asking Allah to grant them a higher place in Paradise.

- It emphasizes that the duties toward parents do not end with their passing but continue through acts of supplication and remembrance.

Hadith 27: Dutifulness After Death: Honoring Parents by Maintaining Their Relationships and Praying for Them

Narrated by Ibn Abbas (may Allah be pleased with him): The Prophet (peace and blessings be upon him) said: "One of the greatest forms of dutifulness is for a man to keep in touch with the loved ones of his father after he has passed away, and to make du'a (supplication) for his parents." (Sunan Ibn Majah, Hadith 3662)

Key Lessons

1. **Maintaining Family and Social Bonds**:

- This hadith emphasizes the importance of maintaining ties with one's father's loved ones and friends after his death. It teaches that honoring one's father's memory involves continuing the relationships and bonds that were important to him.

- Maintaining family and social ties is a form of **birr al-walidayn** (dutifulness to parents), showing that respect for parents extends beyond direct care to include nurturing relationships they value.

2. **Dutifulness to Parents After Death**:
- The hadith stresses that one of the highest forms of honoring one's parents after their death is to make du'a for them. This act of supplication is a key way to show ongoing love and respect for deceased parents, ensuring they continue to benefit from their child's prayers.

- This hadith further emphasizes that the relationship between children and parents endures after death, as children continue to play an essential role in their parents' spiritual well-being.

3. **Maintaining the Legacy of the Deceased**:
- The hadith encourages children to stay connected with their father's loved ones, teaching the value of preserving a parent's legacy through

maintaining the relationships that mattered to them. This is a way of extending the parents' influence and keeping their memory alive.

- It highlights the importance of maintaining a sense of community and honoring the broader social bonds one's parents cultivated during their lifetime.

4. Du'a as a Form of Ongoing Dutifulness:

- Making du'a for parents is presented as a continuous act of dutifulness. Even after parents have passed away, children are encouraged to keep them in their prayers, asking for forgiveness and mercy on their behalf. This shows that parental respect and care are lifelong responsibilities.

- The hadith teaches that the du'a for parents is not only an obligation but also a noble and praiseworthy act that brings immense benefit to both the parents and the children.

Key Lessons from Both Hadiths

1. **Dutifulness to Parents Extends Beyond Death**:

- Both hadiths highlight that dutifulness to parents is not limited to their lifetime. Children can continue to honor their parents by making du'a, seeking forgiveness for them, and maintaining ties with their loved ones, contributing to their parents' spiritual elevation.

2. **The Power of Du'a in Elevating Status in Paradise**:

- Both hadiths underscore the immense power of du'a in benefiting the deceased. Children have a direct impact on their parents' status in the Hereafter by consistently praying for their forgiveness and spiritual well-being, ensuring that their parents are continually elevated in rank.

3. **Maintaining Social Bonds as an Act of Devotion**:

- The second hadith emphasizes the broader concept of **birr al-walidayn**, teaching that children should not only pray for their parents but also maintain the social connections that were important to them. This is seen as a form of devotion that reflects one's respect for their parents' values and relationships.

4. The Continued Responsibility of Children:
- Both hadiths illustrate that children have an ongoing responsibility toward their parents, even after they have passed away. Through supplication and maintaining family ties, children can continue to fulfill their duty toward their parents and ensure their spiritual well-being in the Hereafter.

5. The Compassionate Nature of Allah's Mercy:
- Allah's mercy is reflected in the fact that He allows the deceased to benefit from their children's good deeds. The fact that their children's prayers can elevate parents' status in Paradise shows the far-reaching mercy of Allah, rewarding not only the actions of the individual but also those of their loved ones.

Conclusion

These hadiths emphasize the ongoing responsibility of children to honor their parents through supplication, maintaining social ties, and seeking forgiveness on their behalf. The power of du'a is highlighted as a means to elevate the status of the deceased in Paradise, and children are encouraged to continue fulfilling their duties toward their parents even after death. Maintaining ties with the loved ones of a parent also ensures that their legacy endures and their relationships are respected. These actions reflect the enduring nature of family ties and the mercy of Allah in rewarding the righteous deeds of children for the benefit of their parents.

Chapter 13

The Impact of Treating Parents Well on Children's Lives

Hadith 28: The Blessings of Sustenance and Longevity Through Upholding Family Ties

Narrated by Anas ibn Malik: "Whoever would like his provision to be increased and his lifespan to be extended, let him uphold the ties of kinship." (Sahih al-Bukhari, Book 78, Hadith 12)

Key Lessons

1. **Maintaining Ties of Kinship (Silat al-Rahm)**: This hadith highlights the importance of upholding family connections and kinship ties. Islam places great emphasis on maintaining good relationships with family members, which is seen as a key to earning Allah's blessings.

2. **Increase in Provision and Lifespan**: The hadith promises two significant benefits for those who uphold family ties: an increase in their

provision (sustenance, wealth, or blessings) and an extension of their lifespan. This indicates that maintaining good family relationships has both spiritual and worldly rewards.

3. **Link Between Social and Spiritual Well-being**: The hadith suggests that being connected with family and relatives is a social virtue and one that brings about divine blessings and improves a person's overall quality of life.

Hadith 29: The Reciprocal Blessing of Kindness to Parents

Narrated by Abdullah ibn 'Umar: The Prophet (peace and blessings be upon him) said, "Whoever is kind to his parents, it will be a cause of his children being kind to him." (Al-Mu'jam al-Awsat, Hadith 6062)

Key Lessons

1. **Reciprocity in Parent-Child Relationships**: This hadith teaches that being kind and respectful to one's parents sets an example for future generations. Just as people treat their parents, their children will be inclined to treat them similarly.

2. **Generational Kindness**: It illustrates a natural cycle of behavior within families—kindness toward parents is mirrored by kindness from children. This emphasizes the role of parents in modeling respectful behavior that influences how they themselves will be treated in old age.

3. **Moral and Spiritual Consequences**: The hadith reinforces the idea that one's interactions with one's parents have long-term effects, not only on one's relationship with Allah but also on shaping the dynamics within one's family.

Common Themes:

- **Importance of Family Bonds**: Both hadiths stress the significance of maintaining strong family relationships, whether by upholding kinship ties or showing kindness to parents. Islam encourages mutual care and respect within families to foster harmony and well-being.

- **Divine and Worldly Rewards**: The hadiths link family care and kindness to tangible rewards such as increased provision, longer life, and receiving kindness from one's children. This demonstrates that acts of kindness within the family are rewarded in this life and hereafter.

- **Generational Impact of Kindness:** The second hadith highlights how one's treatment of one's parents can directly influence the behavior of one's children, emphasizing the ripple effect of kindness and respect across generations.

Key Takeaways:

- Upholding kinship ties and being kind to parents are acts that not only bring about divine rewards but also improve one's relationships and life circumstances.

- Respectful and caring treatment of parents sets a positive example for future generations, creating a cycle of kindness and moral behavior within families.

- The connection between family well-being and spiritual blessings underscores Islam's comprehensive approach to family life, where social behavior directly influences both worldly and spiritual outcomes.

In conclusion, these two hadiths emphasize maintaining strong family ties and being kind to parents in Islam. The first hadith illustrates that upholding kinship bonds leads to tangible blessings, such as increased provision and a longer life, showing that family relationships have spiritual and worldly benefits. The second hadith highlights the reciprocal nature of kindness within families, where treating parents well sets an example for one's children to do the same, fostering a cycle of compassion across generations. Together, these hadiths reinforce the Islamic principle that nurturing family relationships is a key to earning Allah's favor, securing blessings in this life, and creating a legacy of kindness and respect within families.

CHAPTER 14

THE GRAVE SIN OF DISOBEDIENCE TO PARENTS

Hadith 30: The Gravest of Major Sins: Shirk and Disobedience to Parents

Narrated by Abu Bakra (may Allah be pleased with him): The Prophet (peace and blessings be upon him) said, "Shall I not tell you the greatest of the major sins?" They said, "Yes, O Messenger of Allah." He said, "Associating partners with Allah, and disobedience to parents." (Sahih al-Bukhari, Hadith 2654)

Key Lessons

1. **Disobedience to Parents as an Unforgivable Sin**: This hadith highlights that disobedience to parents is among the gravest sins, second only to shirk (associating partners with Allah). It emphasizes that this sin will not be forgiven unless there is sincere repentance before death, signifying its immense severity in Islam.

2. **Link Between Shirk and Disobedience to Parents**: The hadith pairs disobedience to parents with shirk, showing that both disrupt

key relationships: shirk disrupts the relationship with Allah, and disobedience to parents disrupts family and societal harmony. These are seen as foundational to one's spiritual and social responsibilities.

Hadith 31: Three Prayers Never Rejected: The Oppressed, the Traveler, and the Parent Against Their Child

Narrated by Abu Hurairah (may Allah be pleased with him): The Prophet (peace and blessings be upon him) said, "Three prayers are answered without a doubt: the prayer of the one who is oppressed, the prayer of the traveler, and the prayer of the parent against his child." (Sunan Ibn Majah, Hadith 3862)

Key Lesson

The du'a (supplication) of a parent, whether for or against their child, is never rejected by Allah. This emphasizes the importance of earning parents' du'as without incurring displeasure.

Hadith 32: Three Sins That Bring Immediate Punishment: Disobedience to Parents, Injustice, and Ingratitude

Narrated by Abdullah ibn Umar (may Allah be pleased with him): The Prophet (peace and blessings be upon him) said: "There are three sins that Allah hastens the punishment for in this world: disobedience to parents, injustice, and ingratitude." (Jami` at-Tirmidhi, Hadith 1898)

Key Lesson

Disobedience to parents is one of the sins for which punishment is hastened in this world, alongside injustice and ingratitude.

Hadith 33: Three People Deprived of Allah's Mercy on the Day of Judgment

Narrated by Abdullah ibn 'Umar: The Prophet (peace and blessings be upon him) said, "There are three types of people whom Allah will not look at on the Day of Judgment: the one who is undutiful to his parents, a woman who imitates men, and a man who does not care about his family's honor (i.e., a cuckold)." (Sunan an-Nasa'i, Book 25, Hadith 3109; Musnad Ahmad, Hadith 5372)

Key Lessons

1. **Severe Consequences for Disobedience to Parents**: This hadith emphasizes the gravity of being undutiful to one's parents. Disobedience to parents is portrayed as a major sin, to the extent that Allah will not even look at such individuals with mercy or favor on the Day of Judgment. This highlights the critical importance of filial piety in Islam.

2. **Gender Roles and Family Honor**: The hadith also addresses two other actions that carry severe spiritual consequences:

- **Women Imitating Men**: It refers to the inappropriate adoption of characteristics, behaviors, or roles that violate Islamic gender norms. This suggests that individuals should respect the distinctions set in Islamic teachings regarding gender.

- **Neglect of Family Honor**: A man who is indifferent to his family's honor (known as *dayyuth*, or "a cuckold") is also included among those whom Allah will not favor on the Day of Judgment. This underscores the importance of upholding moral and ethical standards within the family, particularly concerning modesty and honor.

Common Themes:

- **Severe Consequences of Parental Disobedience**: Both hadiths stress the grave consequences of being undutiful to parents, emphasizing that this is a major sin with spiritual consequences both in this life and the hereafter. Allah's disfavor on the Day of Judgment for those who disobey their parents highlights the seriousness of this act.

- **Core Islamic Values**: The hadiths tie together several core values in Islam: respect and obedience to parents, maintaining family honor and modesty, and upholding proper gender roles. These are linked to maintaining social, spiritual, and familial integrity.

- **Unforgivable Sins**: The hadith from Abdullah ibn Abbas stresses that disobedience to parents is placed alongside shirk as a sin that may not be forgiven without repentance, illustrating how damaging this behavior is in Islam.

Key Takeaways:

- **Filial Piety**: Being dutiful and respectful toward parents is a central tenet of Islamic morality, and failure to uphold this duty is a grave sin that can result in divine punishment on the Day of Judgment.

- **Family Honor and Gender Norms**: In addition to obedience to parents, maintaining family honor and adhering to Islamic gender roles are essential components of Islamic teachings. Failure in these areas can have severe consequences, as demonstrated in these hadiths.

- **Link Between Faith and Family**: The connection between shirk and disobedience to parents shows that Islamic teachings place equal emphasis on one's relationship with Allah and one's relationship with family. Both are foundational to a righteous life in Islam.

In conclusion, these hadiths underscore the profound importance of filial piety and the severe consequences of disobedience to parents in Islam. The first hadith highlights that undutifulness to parents, along with neglecting family honor and violating gender norms, will lead to Allah's disfavor on the Day of Judgment. The second hadith pairs disobedience to parents with shirk, showing that failing to honor one's parents is among the gravest sins, with serious spiritual consequences that may not be forgiven without repentance. Together, these hadiths emphasize that maintaining respect for parents, upholding family values, and preserving modesty are critical to living a righteous life in Islam. Disobeying or neglecting these duties not only disrupts familial harmony but also jeopardizes one's standing before Allah, both in this life and in the hereafter.

Chapter 15

Maintaining Good Relations with Parents' Friends and Relatives

Hadith 34: Honoring Family Legacy: The Righteousness of Kindness to a Father's Friends

Narrated by Abdullah ibn 'Umar (may Allah be pleased with him): Ibn 'Umar (may Allah be pleased with him) was once on a journey when he met a Bedouin man. He greeted him, placed him on his donkey, and gave him a turban that he was wearing on his head. His companions remarked, "May Allah guide you! They are Bedouins, and they would be content with little." Ibn Umar replied, "The father of this man was a friend of my father, and I heard the Messenger of Allah (peace and blessings be upon him) say: 'The best of righteousness is to treat the friends of your father kindly.' (Sahih Muslim, Hadith 2552)

Key Lessons

1. **Continuing Parental Legacy**: This hadith teaches that honoring one's parents extends beyond their death. Maintaining relationships with the

friends of one's parents is a sign of respect and devotion, both to the parent and those they value.

2. **Caring for Family Friends**: Righteousness in Islam involves more than direct acts of worship; it encompasses caring for those connected to our loved ones. Ibn Umar's actions exemplify this broad scope of kindness.

3. **Cultural Sensitivity and Generosity**: Despite the companions' surprise that Bedouins would be content with less, Ibn Umar's generosity highlights the importance of giving without reservation, reflecting a higher standard of respect and honor.

Hadith 35: The Highest Form of Goodness: Maintaining Ties with a Father's Friends After His Death

Narrated by Abdullah ibn 'Umar: The Prophet (peace and blessings be upon him) said, "The finest act of goodness is for a person to maintain ties with his father's friends after he has passed away." (Sahih al-Bukhari, Book 78, Hadith 33)

Key Lessons

1. **Preserving Relationships After Death**: This hadith reinforces the idea that the obligation to honor parents does not end with their death. It extends to their social circle and friends, reflecting a commitment to the values and relationships that were important to them.

2. **Broad Concept of Goodness**: Islam's concept of goodness (birr) is not limited to individual actions, but includes maintaining social and familial ties. Caring for one's parents' friends is part of this larger moral framework.

3. **Sustaining Bonds Across Generations**: This hadith encourages the sustenance of bonds between families across generations. By maintaining these relationships, children uphold their parents' legacy

and continue to nurture the bonds of respect and community.

Hadith 36: The Divine Protection of Kinship Ties: A Promise of Blessing or Severance

Narrated by Abu Huraira: The Prophet (peace and blessings be upon him) said, "Allah created the creation, and when He finished, the womb said, 'At this place, I seek refuge with You from all those who sever me (i.e., cut off ties of kinship).' Allah said, 'Yes, won't you be pleased that I will keep good relations with the one who keeps good relations with you, and I will sever the relation with the one who severs relations with you?' (Sahin al-Bukhari, Book 73, Hadith 16)

Key Lessons

1. **Importance of Kinship (Silat al-Rahm)**: This hadith emphasizes the significance of maintaining ties of kinship. Allah places great importance on family connections, and severing those ties is considered a major sin.

2. **Divine Blessing for Maintaining Kinship**: Allah promises to keep good relations with those who uphold family ties, offering them divine favor and blessings. Conversely, those who break kinship bonds face the consequences of Allah severing His relationship with them, which indicates the serious spiritual consequences of cutting off family ties.

3. The metaphor of the Womb (Rahm): The hadith metaphorically connects the womb (Rahm) to the concept of family bonds, highlighting the natural connection between family members. The use of the womb emphasizes the deeply rooted, intrinsic nature of family relationships and the protection they deserve in Islamic teachings.

Common Themes:

- **Continuing Goodness and Respect After Death**: Both hadiths emphasize that the duty to respect and honor family and relationships continues beyond the lifetime of one's parents. Whether by maintaining ties with a father's friends or preserving kinship ties, these actions reflect ongoing goodness and fulfill one's responsibilities toward family.

- Divine Favor and Punishment Related to Family Bonds: The second hadith connects maintaining family ties with divine favor while severing those ties lead to Allah's disfavor. This highlights that kinship is not merely a social obligation but a spiritual one with significant consequences.

- **Social and Family Bonds as Extensions of Faith**: Both hadiths illustrate that one's relationships with others—whether friends of a deceased parent or extended family members—are critical components of a believer's ethical and spiritual life. Family and social relationships are viewed as sacred and must be preserved.

Key Takeaways:

- Islam places great emphasis on honoring parents, not only through direct service but also by respecting their friendships and continuing these relationships after they pass away.

- Maintaining kinship ties is central to Islamic ethics, as breaking those ties can lead to spiritual consequences and loss of divine favor while preserving them brings Allah's blessings.

- Both hadiths reflect the broader Islamic principle that family and social bonds are integral to one's faith and moral conduct, and these relationships must be upheld as a means of earning Allah's pleasure.

In conclusion, these hadiths highlight the significant role of family and social relationships in Islam, emphasizing that honoring parents and maintaining kinship ties extend beyond immediate interactions. The first hadith teaches that even after a parent's death, continuing relationships with their friends is an act of great goodness, reflecting ongoing respect and loyalty to the deceased. The second hadith underscores the critical importance of preserving family ties, with a promise of Allah's blessings for those who uphold kinship and a warning of His displeasure for those who sever them. Together, these teachings stress that family bonds and social connections are not only social responsibilities but also spiritual obligations that have profound implications for one's relationship with Allah. Maintaining these bonds is key to righteousness and earning divine favor in this life and the hereafter.

Chapter 16

Giving Charity on Behalf of Deceased Parents

Hadith 37: Charity for a Deceased Parent: The Continuing Benefit of Acts of Kindness

Abdullah Ibn Abbas narrated that Saad bin Ubadah said: "O Messenger of Allah, my mother has died while I was away from her. Will it benefit her if I give charity on her behalf?" The Prophet (peace and blessings be upon him) said: "Yes." So Saad said: "I bear witness that my two sheepfolds are a charity for her." (Sahih al-Bukhari, Hadith 2760; Sunan Abu Dawood: Hadith 2880)

Key Lesson

This hadith emphasizes that deeds done by a living person can benefit a deceased person, particularly in the form of *sadaqah jariya* (continuous charity). Sadaqah Jariyah refers to charity that provides ongoing benefits even after the person has passed away. In this case, Saad's charity would continue to benefit his mother after her death.

Hadith 38: Posthumous Charity: A Mother's Reward Through Her Child's Giving

Aisha (may Allah be pleased with her) reported that a man said to the Prophet (peace and blessings be upon him):
"My mother died suddenly, and I think that if she had spoken (before her death), she would have given in charity. Will she be rewarded if I give in charity on her behalf?" The Prophet (peace and blessings be upon him) replied, "Yes." (Sahih al-Bukhari, Book 55, Hadith 19)

Explanation

This Hadith emphasizes that giving charity on behalf of a deceased parent is an ongoing source of blessings for them, even after they have passed away. It highlights how children can continue to benefit their parents in the Hereafter. The concept of *sadaqah jariyah* (continuous charity) is a cornerstone of Islamic ethics, where certain acts—such as charity—continue to accrue rewards for the individual even after their death.

Key Lessons

1. **Charity Benefits Deceased Parents**: Both hadiths confirm that charity given on behalf of a deceased parent benefits them. The Prophet (peace and blessings be upon him) affirmed that such charitable acts bring rewards to the deceased, emphasizing that children can continue to support their parents' spiritual well-being after their death.

2. **Ongoing Responsibility Towards Deceased Parents**: The hadiths demonstrate that a child's duty to their parents extends beyond their lifetime. Through acts like charity, children can continue to honor their parents and provide them with ongoing rewards, showing that filial piety in Islam persists even after death.

3. **Charity as a Form of *Sadaqah Jariyah* (Ongoing Charity)**: Charity

on behalf of the deceased is viewed as *sadaqah jariyah*, which means ongoing charity that benefits the giver and the recipient even after death. This highlights the lasting impact of charitable deeds and how they can be a source of ongoing rewards in the hereafter.

4. **Intention and Fulfillment of Parental Wishes**: In both cases, the children acted based on their belief that their deceased parents would have given charity if they had the chance. The Prophet's approval shows that fulfilling what a child believes their parent would have done is valid and highly rewarding, especially when it aligns with good deeds like charity.

5. **Proactive Approach to Benefit the Deceased**: These hadiths encourage a proactive approach to seeking benefits for deceased parents. Rather than passively mourning, children are encouraged to take actions that bring ongoing benefits to their parents in the hereafter, such as through charity and good deeds.

6. **Connection Between Parent and Child**: The deep bond between parent and child continues after death, and through acts of kindness and charity, a child can still affect their parent's spiritual status. This reinforces the strong connection between family members and the importance of maintaining that relationship even in the afterlife.

Common Themes:

- **Continuity of Good Deeds**: Children can extend their parents' good deeds after death, ensuring their legacy of charity and goodness continues.

- **Charity as a Lifelong Benefit**: Giving charity on parents' behalf is a way to honor them and provide them with spiritual rewards in the afterlife.

- **Filial Piety Beyond Death**: Islam encourages honoring parents not only in life but also after death through acts of charity and other righteous deeds, reflecting the ongoing importance of parental rights.

Key Takeaways:

- **Charity on behalf of the deceased**: These hadiths illustrate the importance and effectiveness of giving charity on behalf of a deceased parent, providing them with rewards in the afterlife.

- **Ongoing duty to parents**: Children have a continued responsibility to honor and benefit their parents through acts of kindness and charity, even after their passing.

- **Charity as a source of lasting reward**: Charitable deeds performed in the name of deceased parents act as *sadaqah jariyah*, offering ongoing benefits in this life and the hereafter.

In conclusion, these hadiths emphasize that a child's responsibility to honor and benefit their parents extends beyond their lifetime. Charity given on behalf of deceased parents is not only permissible but highly beneficial, providing them with ongoing rewards in the hereafter. This reinforces the concept of *sadaqah jariyah* (ongoing charity) and the importance of performing righteous deeds that continue to benefit both the living and the deceased. The teachings highlight the deep and enduring connection between parent and child, encouraging children to take proactive steps, such as giving charity, honoring their parents, and securing rewards for them even after their passing. This exemplifies the comprehensive nature of filial piety in Islam, where the relationship between parents and children transcends life and death.

Chapter 17

The Influence of Parents' Supplications

Hadith 39: Three Supplications Always Answered: The Oppressed, the Traveler, and the Parent's Du'a for Their Child

Abu Hurairah (may Allah be pleased with him) reported that the Prophet Muhammad (peace and blessings be upon him) said: "Three supplications are surely accepted without doubt: The prayer of one who is oppressed, the prayer of a traveler, and the prayer of a parent for their child." (Sunan Ibn Majah, Book 34, Hadith 3862)

Key Lessons

1. **The Special Status of Parental Supplication**: The hadith emphasizes the special weight and importance that the supplication (du'a) of parents holds in the sight of Allah. Among the three supplications mentioned—those of the oppressed, the traveler, and the parent—the du'a of a parent for their child is singled out as one that is **surely**

accepted without doubt. This reflects the unique bond between parents and children and underscores how Allah honors and elevates the sincere prayers made by parents for their offspring.

2. **Parents' Supplications Shape a Child's Destiny**: A parent's supplication for their child can have a profound effect on the child's life. Whether the du'a is for guidance, protection, success, or well-being, parents' du'as are powerful in shaping their children's physical and spiritual state. This hadith teaches that parents should be mindful and consistent in making positive, heartfelt du'a for their children, as it can open the doors to divine blessings and protection throughout their child's life.

3. **The Parental Role in Spiritual Guidance**: This hadith highlights the spiritual responsibility parents have for their children, not just in terms of upbringing but also in supplicating for their moral and spiritual development. It reminds parents that beyond physical care and provision, they have the ability to positively influence their children's lives through regular and sincere supplication. This is particularly important during challenging times, where a parent's du'a can provide comfort and divine intervention.

4. **Divine Mercy and Parental Love**: The hadith shows that Allah's mercy is closely connected to the compassion and care parents feel for their children. The fact that parents' du'as are accepted without doubt highlights the depth of mercy and love Allah has placed within the parent-child relationship. Parental love reflects divine mercy, and accepting their supplication is a testament to how much Allah values this bond.

5. **Encouragement for Children to Seek Parents' Du'a**: This hadith reminds children of the immense value of seeking their parents' du'as and blessings. Since the du'a of a parent is so readily accepted, children should try to earn their parents' love, respect, and supplications. It emphasizes the importance of honoring one's parents, not only as

a religious obligation but as a means of gaining Allah's favor and protection through their supplications.

6. **Parental Du'a as a Form of Spiritual Legacy**: This hadith also teaches that the du'a of a parent is a lasting form of spiritual care and legacy. Even when a parent is no longer physically present, their du'as can continue to bring blessings and protection to their children. It encourages parents to make du'a not just for their children's current needs but also for their long-term success, righteousness, and faith.

Hadith 40: A Father's Du'a: As Powerful as a Prophet's Supplication for His People

Narrated by Abdullah ibn Abbas: The Prophet (peace and blessings be upon him) said, "A father's supplication for his child is like a prophet's du'a for his people." (Tabarani in Al-Mu'jam al-Awsat, Hadith 6067)

Key Lessons

1. **The Power of a Father's Du'a**: The hadith compares the du'a of a father for his child to the du'a of a prophet for his people, highlighting the immense power and impact a father's supplication holds. Just as a prophet's du'a is sincere and heartfelt and carries weight before Allah, so is a father's du'a for his child. This underscores the unique spiritual significance of a father's du'as in shaping the destiny and well-being of his children.

2. **Parental Responsibility in Spiritual Guidance**: The comparison to a prophet's du'a shows that, like prophets who care deeply for their people's spiritual and worldly success, a father has a similar responsibility for his child. The father's role is not limited to providing for the physical needs of his children; he also plays a crucial role in their spiritual development through his du'as and guidance. This hadith encourages

fathers to actively support their children's success in this life and the Hereafter.

3. **The Blessings of a Father's Du'a**: Just as the du'a of a prophet brings blessings, protection, and guidance to their community, the father's du'a brings divine blessings and protection to his children. This shows how a father's sincere and regular supplications can be a source of ongoing goodness, safety, and divine intervention in his child's life.

4. **A Father's Love and Mercy**: The analogy to a prophet's du'a reflects a father's deep love, care, and mercy for his child. Prophets supplicate for their people with immense compassion, seeking their well-being in worldly and spiritual matters. Similarly, a father's du'a expresses his unconditional love, concern, and desire for his child's success. This hadith highlights that the father-child relationship is one of mercy and care, deeply valued in Islam.

5. **Encouragement for Children to Seek Their Father's Du'a**: Just as the people seek a prophet's du'a, this hadith implies that children should seek their father's du'a, understanding its immense value and impact. A father's du'a can open the doors to divine mercy and guidance, and children are encouraged to maintain a strong relationship with their fathers and request their du'as, especially in times of need.

6. **Spiritual Authority of Fathers**: The comparison to a prophet also indicates the spiritual authority and responsibility that fathers carry. Like prophets who are trusted to guide their people, fathers are entrusted with their children's spiritual and moral upbringing. This hadith reminds fathers of their duty to supplicate for and guide their children, knowing their supplication holds great weight before Allah.

Common Themes:

- **Powerful Status of Parental Supplications**: Both hadiths highlight that a parent's supplication for their child is uniquely powerful and guaranteed acceptance by Allah, similar to the du'as of the oppressed and the traveler.

- **Parental Responsibility in Spiritual Leadership**: Parents are not only responsible for their children's upbringing in a worldly sense but are also seen as spiritual guardians whose du'as carry immense significance.

- **Divine Favor Toward Parental Love**: The special acceptance of parental du'as reflects the value Allah places on the natural love and care parents have for their children. This serves as a testament to the mercy and compassion that characterize the parent-child relationship in Islam.

Key Takeaways:

- **Parental du'a is a powerful tool**: Parents are encouraged to make sincere du'as for their children, as these du'ass hold a special status with Allah and are guaranteed to be accepted.

- **Parents as spiritual guides**: A parent's role extends beyond physical care to spiritual leadership, where their du'a for their children can have long-lasting effects, similar to the du'a of a prophet for his people.

- **Strength of unconditional love**: The deep love and concern parents have for their children are recognized and honored by Allah, as reflected in the guaranteed acceptance of their supplications for their children's well-being and success.

In conclusion, these hadiths highlight the profound power and significance of a parent's supplication for their child in Islam. A parent's du'a is guaranteed acceptance by Allah, reflecting parents' deep love, care, and responsibility for their children's spiritual and worldly well-being. The comparison of a father's du'as to that of a prophet for his people emphasizes the spiritual leadership role parents hold within the family. These teachings encourage parents to make sincere du'a for their children, recognizing that their du'as are a form of guidance and protection and a vital means of securing Allah's blessings for their children's success in this life and the hereafter. Ultimately, the parent-child relationship is elevated as one filled with divine favor, where parental love is a powerful source of mercy and guidance.

Chapter 18

The Role of Parents in Leading Children to Righteousness

Hadith 41: Responsibility of Leadership: Every Individual is a Shepherd of Their Own Flock

Narrated by Abdullah ibn 'Umar: "The Prophet (peace and blessings be upon him) said: 'Every one of you is a shepherd and is responsible for his flock. The leader of a people is a shepherd and is responsible for his subjects. A man is the shepherd of his family and is responsible for them. A woman is the shepherd of her husband's home and his children and is responsible for them. The servant of a man is a shepherd of his master's wealth and is responsible for it. So each one of you is a shepherd and is responsible for his flock.'" (Sahih al-Bukhari, Book 93, Hadith 3; Sahih Muslim, Book 33, Hadith 20)

Key Lessons

1. **Universal Responsibility**: This hadith highlights the principle that every individual has a role of responsibility, regardless of their position in

society. Everyone is accountable for those under their care or authority, whether a leader, parent, spouse, or servant.

2. **Leadership in Different Contexts**: The hadith emphasizes that leadership and responsibility are not limited to political or formal roles. A man's responsibility is toward his family, a woman's responsibility lies in caring for the home and children, and even a servant has a duty to manage their master's wealth with care. This shows that leadership is multifaceted and exists in every aspect of life.

3. **Accountability Before Allah**: Each person's "flock" refers to those they are responsible for, and Allah will hold them accountable for how they manage their duties. This hadith encourages vigilance, responsibility, and justice in all spheres of life.

4. **Balanced Responsibility for Men and Women**: Both men and women are recognized as "shepherds" with specific duties toward their families. Men are tasked with the broader care of the family, while women are entrusted with maintaining the household and raising children. This highlights that both genders have distinct but equally important roles in the family structure.

Hadith 42: The Greatest Gift: A Father's Legacy of Good Manners

Narrated by Amr ibn Sa'id: The Prophet (peace and blessings be upon him) said, "No father can give his child anything better than good manners" (Jami' at-Tirmidhi, Book 27, Hadith 33 / Hadith 1952 in some collections)

Key Lessons

1. **Importance of Good Manners**: This hadith highlights that one of the greatest gifts a parent can give their child is teaching good manners.

Good character and conduct are prioritized over material wealth, as they shape the child's moral foundation and future behavior.

2. **Manners as a Lifelong Asset**: Teaching children good manners equips them with essential tools for life, enabling them to build strong relationships, behave with integrity, and contribute positively to society. This emphasizes the role of parents in instilling values such as respect, kindness, and empathy in their children.

- **Moral and Spiritual Education**: The hadith underscores the idea that character development is essential to a parent's responsibility. Parents should focus on nurturing their children's inner qualities, which will have lasting benefits both in this life and in the hereafter.

Hadith 43: Excellence Begins at Home: The Best Among You Are Best to Their Families

Narrated by Abdullah ibn Abbas: The Prophet (peace and blessings be upon him) said, "The best of you are those who are best to their families, and I am the best of you to my family." (Sunan ibn Majah, Book 33, Hadith 1977)

Key Lessons

1. **Excellence Begins at Home**: This hadith emphasizes that the true measure of a person's character is how they treat their family. Being kind, supportive, and loving toward one's family members reflects a person's integrity and goodness.

2. **The Prophet's Example**: The Prophet Muhammad (peace and blessings be upon him) is the best example of how to treat one's family. He demonstrated that personal conduct with loved ones is a core aspect of Islamic values. His compassion, respect, and care for his family provide a model for all Muslims.

3. **Family as a Primary Responsibility**: This hadith underscores that while public conduct is important, a person's true character is revealed at home. Treating one's family with kindness, fairness, and respect reflects true righteousness.

Lessons from the Hadiths

1. Parents Are Role Models and Guides for Their Children:

- The hadith comparing each individual to a shepherd emphasizes that **parents have a critical role as guides and protectors** of their children. Just as a shepherd is responsible for the safety and well-being of their flock, parents are responsible for the physical, emotional, and spiritual well-being of their children.

- This role involves ensuring children are raised with Islamic values, moral character, and good manners, as demonstrated by the guidance from the Prophet (peace be upon him). Parents serve as both role models and caretakers of their children's faith and ethical development.

2. Moral and Spiritual Development is a Key Responsibility:

- The hadith on giving children good manners highlights that **instilling good character and ethical behavior** is one of the most important gifts parents can give their children. It is more valuable than wealth or material success because it prepares children to live righteously and be responsible members of society.

- Parents are tasked with teaching children honesty, kindness, patience, respect, and other values that are foundational to Islam. This hadith emphasizes that moral and spiritual upbringing is the greatest inheritance a child can receive.

3. Nurturing a Loving and Supportive Family Environment:

- The hadith of being the best for one's family highlights the importance of **creating a loving, compassionate, and supportive home environment**. The Prophet Muhammad (peace and blessings be upon him) led by example in being kind and caring toward his own family, showing that parents should not only be disciplinarians but also sources of love and compassion.

- This hadith teaches that the way a parent treats their family is a direct reflection of their character. Children learn from how their parents interact with them and others in the household. By modeling kindness and respect, parents instill these values in their children.

4. Parents' Accountability Before Allah:
- The "shepherd" hadith stresses that parents are accountable for their children's spiritual and moral upbringing. Allah will question them about how they nurtured and guided their children. This responsibility encourages parents to be vigilant and active in ensuring their children develop righteous character and live according to Islamic principles.

- Being responsible for one's "flock" includes protecting children from harmful influences, teaching them the values of Islam, and helping them grow into responsible and ethical adults.

5. Good Manners are the Foundation of Righteousness:
- The hadith on good manners emphasizes that **good character is the cornerstone of Islamic teachings**. Parents are responsible for teaching their children adab (proper manners) in every aspect of life, including how to treat others with respect, kindness, and dignity.

- This hadith reminds parents that education and training in good manners are crucial for a child's success in this life and the Hereafter. It also emphasizes that a well-mannered child reflects the parents' efforts and guidance.

6. Parental Compassion and Justice:
- The hadith, "the best of you are those who are best to their families,"

teaches parents to practice compassion, justice, and fairness within their families. How parents treat their children and other family members directly impacts the children's perception of righteousness, justice, and ethical behavior.

- This hadith stresses the importance of treating children with love and fairness, ensuring that the family home is a place of peace, security, and moral guidance.

7. Parents' Influence on Long-Term Character Development:
- These hadiths collectively highlight the **long-term impact parents have on their children's development**. Children raised with love, good manners, and strong Islamic values are more likely to grow into righteous and responsible adults who contribute positively to their communities.

- The role of the parent is not only to provide for their children in the material sense but also to **guide them toward being ethical, compassionate, and God-conscious individuals**.

8. Family as the Foundation of Society:
- The "shepherd" hadith indicates that families are the building blocks of a righteous society. If parents fulfill their responsibilities effectively by instilling good values and guiding their children toward righteousness, they help create a strong, ethical community.

- Children raised in families that embody Islamic teachings of love, respect, and responsibility are more likely to become positive influences in society.

Conclusion

These hadiths emphasize the **critical role of parents as the primary moral and spiritual guides** for their children. Parents are responsible for raising children with good manners, strong Islamic values, and a loving, supportive environment. They are role models, shaping their children's character and leading them toward righteousness. By fulfilling these responsibilities, parents secure their children's well-being and contribute to building a just and ethical society. The hadiths remind parents of the profound accountability they hold before Allah for the upbringing of their children, encouraging them to be active and compassionate shepherds of their families.

Chapter 19

Honoring and Treating Parents with Excellence in the Quran

The Qur'an emphasizes kindness and respect towards parents, portraying it as one of the most important aspects of a believer's relationship with others. The teachings repeatedly emphasize the need for compassion, understanding, and support for parents, especially in their old age. Below are some key verses from the Qur'an regarding kindness to parents, along with an analysis of each.

1. Surah Al-Isra (17:23-24)

"And your Lord has decreed that you worship none but Him and be kind to parents. Whether one or both of them reach old age while with you, say not to them [so much as], 'uff,' and do not repel them but speak to them a noble word. And lower to them the wing of humility out of mercy and say, 'My Lord, have mercy upon them as they brought me up [when I was] small.'" (Qur'an 17:23-24)

This verse emphasizes two crucial commandments from Allah: worship Him alone and be kind to parents. The Qur'an highlights its immense importance by placing kindness in parents immediately after the obligation to worship Allah.

The prohibition against saying "uff" (a term expressing the slightest annoyance) shows that even the smallest disrespect toward parents is unacceptable. Instead, believers are instructed to speak kindly and humble themselves before their parents, especially in their old age. The prayer for parents ("My Lord, have mercy upon them...") reflects the acknowledgment of their sacrifices and the need to continually seek Allah's mercy for them.

2. Surah Luqman (31:14-15)

"And We have enjoined upon man [care] for his parents. His mother carried him, [increasing her] in weakness upon weakness, and his weaning is in two years. Be grateful to Me and your parents; to Me is the [final] destination. But if they endeavor to make you associate with Me that of which you have no knowledge, do not obey them but accompany them in [this] world with appropriate kindness and follow the way of those who turn back to Me [in repentance]. Then to Me will be your return, and I will inform you about what you used to do." (Qur'an 31:14-15)

This verse emphasizes the mother's struggles, noting the challenges of pregnancy, childbirth, and nursing, highlighting her sacrifices to create a sense of gratitude. Allah commands believers to be grateful both to Him and to their parents. Even in cases where parents may instruct their children toward actions that go against faith, the children are not allowed to be rude or disrespectful. Instead, they are commanded to treat their parents with kindness while politely declining to obey in matters that contradict Allah's commands. This shows a balanced approach to filial piety and adherence to faith.

3. Surah Al-Ankabut (29:8)

"And We have enjoined upon man goodness to parents. But if they endeavor to make you associate with Me that of which you have no knowledge, do not obey them. To Me is your return, and I will inform you about what you used to do." (Qur'an 29:8)

This verse reiterates the obligation of kindness to parents but also sets a boundary regarding faith. If parents encourage actions that involve shirk (associating partners with Allah), the child must not obey them, but this disobedience should be done respectfully. It underscores the principle of respecting parents while maintaining unwavering faith in Allah.

4. Surah Al-Ahqaf (46:15)

"And We have enjoined upon man, to his parents, good treatment. His mother carried him with hardship and gave birth to him with hardship, and his gestation and weaning [period] is thirty months. [He grows]until, when he reaches maturity and reaches [the age of]forty years, he says, 'My Lord, enable me to be grateful for Your favor which you have bestowed upon and upon my parents and to work righteousness of which You will approve and make righteous for me my offspring. Indeed, I have repented to You, and indeed, I am of the Muslims.'" (Qur'an 46:15)

This verse emphasizes the sacrifices of mothers in carrying and nurturing their children, again highlighting the importance of gratitude. When a person reaches maturity, they are encouraged to recognize the blessings from Allah and their parents, and they pray for the ability to be righteous and grateful and for the well-being of their offspring. This verse connects the stages of life, showing that just as parents sacrifice for their children, those children must grow to acknowledge and honor those sacrifices.

5. Surah Al-An'am (6:151)

"Say, 'Come, I will recite what your Lord has prohibited to you. He commands that you not associate anything with Him, and to parents, good treatment...'" (Qur'an 6:151)

In this verse, Allah lists fundamental prohibitions and commands. After the prohibition of shirk (associating partners with Allah), the commandment to treat parents well is mentioned, reinforcing the importance of this duty. The placement of kindness to parents immediately after the command to worship Allah alone signifies its high fundamental prohibitions and commandments. After the prohibition of shirk(associating partners with Allah), the commandment to treat parents well is mentioned, reinforcing the importance of this duty. The placement of kindness to parents immediately after the command to worship Allah alone signifies its high status in Islamic teachings.

6. Surah Maryam (19:14-15) - About Prophet Yahya (John)

"And [he was] dutiful to his parents, and he was not a disobedient tyrant. And peace be upon him the day he was born and the day he dies and the day he is raised alive." (Qur'an 19:14-15)

This verse refers to Prophet Yahya (peace be upon him) and describes his character as dutiful to his parents. The verse also highlights that Yahya was neither arrogant nor rebellious, that humility and obedience to parents earn divine favor, and that being dutiful to parents is a quality of righteous individuals beloved to Allah.

7. Surah Maryam (19:32) - About Prophet Isa

"[Isa said], 'And [He has made me] dutiful to my mother, and He has not made me a wretched tyrant.'" (Qur'an 19:32)

In this verse, Prophet Isa (peace be upon him)speaks of being made dutiful to his mother. This reflects the importance of honoring one's mother and humility. The contrast with being a "wretched tyrant" emphasizes that neglecting or disrespecting one's parents is akin to being a tyrant, while true righteousness is found in compassion and care for them.

Summary of Quranic Teachings on Kindness to Parents

1. Importance of Worship and Kindness: The Qur'an repeatedly places kindness to parents immediately after the command to worship Allah, highlighting its significance (17:23, 6:151).

2. Respect and Humility: Believers are taught to lower their wings of humility towards parents, speak gently to them, and never express even the slightest annoyance (17:23-24).

3. Mothers' Sacrifices: Special mention is made of mothers and the hardships they endure in pregnancy, childbirth, and nursing, which require gratitude from the child (31:14, 46:15).

4. Limits of Obedience: Parents are to be treated with kindness, and children are not obliged to obey them in matters involving shirk or disobedience to Allah, yet they must still be respectful (31:15, 29:8).

5. Supplication for Parents: Believers are encouraged to supplicate for their parents, asking Allah to have mercy upon them and acknowledging their sacrifices (17:24, 46:15).

6. Prophets as Examples: The dutiful behavior of prophets like Yahya and Isa (peace be upon them) towards their parents is a model for all believers (19:14, 19:32).

These teachings collectively underline the central role of parents in an individual's life and the immense value placed on honoring them. Being dutiful to one's parents is the way of the prophets and is portrayed as a reflection of faith, an act of gratitude, and a way to earn Allah's pleasure and mercy.

Chapter 20

Acts of Kindness Toward Parents: Inspiring Examples from Early Muslims

The early Muslims (the Salaf) exhibited remarkable kindness, respect, and devotion toward their parents, setting standards of excellence in filial piety. Here are some notable stories of early Muslims that demonstrate their exceptional treatment of their parents and the status they earned because of it.

1. Uwais al-Qarni: A Model of Devotion

Uwais al-Qarni was a well-known figure from Yemen who lived during the time of Prophet Muhammad (peace and blessings be upon him) but never met him because he cared for his ill mother. He prioritized serving his mother despite having a strong desire to meet the Prophet, a choice that earned him special recognition. The Prophet (peace and blessings be upon him) said about Uwais:

"There will come to you, Uwais ibn Amir, with reinforcements from the people of Yemen. He was suffering from leprosy, but he was cured of it except for a spot as large as a dirham. He has a mother to whom he is very devoted. If he swears by Allah (to do something), Allah will fulfill his oath. If you can ask him to pray for your forgiveness, do." (Sahih Muslim)

Uwais al-Qarni's devotion to his mother was so profound that the Prophet (peace and blessings be upon him) mentioned him specifically, and his prayers were recommended to others. This story demonstrates that prioritizing parents over even noble goals, such as meeting the Prophet (peace and blessings be upon him), holds immense value. His mother's needs were more important to him than personal aspirations, so he earned a high spiritual status.

2. Abdullah ibn Umar: Reverence After Death

After the passing of his father, Caliph Umar ibn al-Khattab, Abdullah ibn Umar was known for his consistent kindness to his father's friends and his dedication to maintaining their ties. Once, while traveling, Abdullah met a Bedouin man. He offered the man his donkey to ride and gave him his turban. When asked by his companions why he was treating the man so generously, Abdullah replied:

"The man's father was a friend of my father, and I heard the Messenger of Allah (peace and blessings be upon him) say: 'One of the best acts of righteousness is for the son to uphold ties with his father's friends.'" (Sahih Muslim)

Abdullah ibn 'Umar understood that honoring his parents went beyond their lifetime. His reverence for his late father's friends demonstrated his respect for his father even after his death. This story reflects that being good to parents is a lifelong commitment that includes maintaining their relationships.

3. Abu Huraira: Carrying His Mother

Abu Huraira, one of the Prophet's (peace and blessings be upon him) closest companions and the most prolific narrator of hadith, was known for his deep respect and care for his mother. He often prayed for her and would always try to make her happy. It is narrated that Abu Huraira's joy knew no bounds when his mother accepted Islam. He used to say:

"I called my mother to Islam when she was a polytheist. One day, I invited her, and she said something about the Prophet (peace and blessings be upon him) that saddened me. I went to the Messenger of Allah weeping and said: 'O Messenger of Allah, I kept calling my mother to Islam, and she kept refusing. Today, I called her again, and she said something saddened me. Pray to Allah to guide the mother of AbuHuraira.' The Messenger of Allah said, 'O Allah, guide the mother of AbuHuraira.' So I went out with joy and returned, finding the door closed. My mother said, 'Wait!' and I heard the water splashing. She then put on her garment and came out saying,' I testify that none has the right to be worshipped except Allah, and Muhammad is His servant and Messenger.'" (Sahih Muslim)

Abu Huraira's dedication to his mother and constant efforts to call her to Islam show the depth of his devotion. His care was not just in fulfilling her physical needs but also in deeply desiring her spiritual well-being. His happiness at her acceptance of Islam illustrates the fulfillment that children derive from their parents' well-being.

4. Ali ibn Abi Talib: Respecting Fatimah bint Asad

Ali ibn Abi Talib, the cousin and son-in-law of the Prophet (peace and blessings be upon him), was deeply devoted to his mother, Fatimah bint Asad. She was the woman who raised him when his father faced difficulties, and he showed her profound respect. When she passed, the Prophet Muhammad (peace and blessings be upon him) himself participated in her burial, and he prayed for her, saying:

"May Allah have mercy on you, O mother of Ali. You were to me like my own mother. You used to go hungry yourself to feed me, go without clothes yourself to provide me with clothes, and refrain from eating good food so that I could eat it."

Fatimah bint Asad's sacrifices were deeply acknowledged by the Prophet (peace and blessings be upon him), which reflects the gratitude Ali and others had for her. Ali's reverence for her and his adherence to her needs were pivotal examples of love for a parent figure, emphasizing how respect and kindness are not just for biological parents but also for those who take on that role.

5. Zain ul-Abidin: The Pious Son of Hussain ibn Ali

Zain ul-Abidin, also known as Aliibn al-Hussain, was the great-grandson of the Prophet Muhammad (peace and blessings be upon him) and was famous for his piety. He was particularly well-known for his incredible treatment of his mother. He was one of the most devoted children to his mother, but he would not eat with her. When asked why, he said:

"I fear my hand may reach for a piece of food she was already reaching for, which would be disrespectful."

This story illustrates the incredible level of care and attention that Zain ul-Abidin gave to honoring his mother. He went to extraordinary lengths to ensure he never inadvertently showed her the slightest disrespect. His behavior represents an ideal of respect that considers even the smallest gestures, reflecting the deep consciousness and care a child should have for their parents.

Summary

These stories of early Muslims highlight how, through prioritizing their parents over personal desires, maintaining their relationships after their passing, ensuring emotional and spiritual well-being, or providing physical comfort, these figures exemplify the highest standards of filial piety. They showed respect, love, and devotion to their parents.

The legacy of the early Muslims teaches us that kindness to parents is not just a duty but a pathway to Allah's pleasure and blessings. Their actions were rewarded in their lives and beyond, demonstrating that the honor given to parents is not merely a cultural value but a deeply spiritual obligation with profound benefits.

CHAPTER 21

KINDNESS TO PARENTS: EXEMPLARY STORIES FROM LATER GENERATIONS OF MUSLIMS

Muslims from later generations have continued to set remarkable examples of kindness and devotion towards their parents, which has often resulted in Allah elevating their status in this world and hereafter. Here are some inspiring stories from notable figures in Islamic history:

1. Imam Abu Hanifa: Serving His Mother with Dedication

Imam Abu Hanifa, the founder of the Hanafi school of Islamic jurisprudence, was known for his deep knowledge and wisdom and his immense respect for his mother. Imam Abu Hanifa's mother sometimes had religious questions, and even though her son was among the most knowledgeable scholars of the time, she insisted on hearing the answers from a particular local scholar named Al-Qasim. Despite his own eminence, Abu Hanifa would take his mother to Al-Qasim to address her concerns, even if the answers were sometimes ones he knew himself.

Abu Hanifa's respect for his mother's wishes, despite his superior knowledge, shows the humility he exhibited in front of his mother. His actions reflect a deep understanding of the importance of honoring one's parents, placing their comfort and emotional needs above personal pride or convenience. His status in the scholarly community is also seen as a reflection of his piety, which includes his treatment of his mother.

2. Rabi'a al-Adawiyya: Dutifulness to Parents and Elevated Spiritual Status

Rabi'a al-Adawiyya, a renowned female mystic from Basra, was known for her spiritual devotion and selflessness. Before becoming a famous ascetic, she was known for her dedication to serving her parents. Being the youngest of her siblings and from a poor family, Rabi'a did whatever she could to make her parents comfortable, even going hungry to provide for them.

Rabia's devotion and selflessness towards her parents contributed to her high spiritual status, and Allah blessed her with an elevated rank among the saints of Islamic history. Her spiritual wisdom, deep love for Allah, and high devotion are believed to be rewards for her early kindness and sacrifices for her family.

3. Imam Al-Shafi'i: Honoring His Mother

Imam Al-Shafi'i, the founder of the Shafi'i School of Thought, was known for his love and care for his mother. He was raised by his mother alone after his father passed away while he was still young. Imam Al-Shafi'i would travel extensively to acquire knowledge, but despite pursuing education, he never neglected his duty towards his mother. It is narrated that he would serve her tirelessly whenever he was home, ensuring her needs were met before even tending to his own.

Imam Al-Shafi'i's devotion to his mother earned him Allah's favor, elevating his status as one of the greatest scholars in Islamic history. His life story demonstrates that dedication to parents does not hinder one's personal or spiritual growth; instead, it becomes a means of earning Allah's barakah (blessings).

4. Muhammad ibn Sirin: Exceptional Kindness to His Mother

Muhammad ibn Sirin, one of the prominent figures in early Islamic history known for his piety and knowledge, treated his mother with immense respect. It is said that whenever he spoke to his mother, he would lower his voice and sit in a humble posture. Even when engaging in discussions of serious scholarship or business, he would excuse himself if his mother called, regardless of the importance of the conversation.

Muhammad ibn Sirin's devotion and respect for his mother were directly linked to his elevated spiritual and moral standing in the community. Allah blessed him with the special gift of interpreting dreams accurately, which was widely regarded as an honor bestowed upon him due to his righteousness, of which his kindness to his mother was a central part.

5. Sufyan Al-Thawri: Prioritizing His Mother's Needs

Sufyan Al-Thawri, a well-known scholar and one of the founders of an early school of jurisprudence, was also known for his dutifulness toward his mother. Despite his deep involvement in scholarship, Sufyan would never let his pursuits compromise the care of his mother. He often said that his mother's well-being precedes all other commitments. His mother used to tell him: "O my son, seek knowledge, and I will suffice you with my spinning wheel," meaning she would take care of their financial needs if he focused on acquiring religious knowledge.

Sufyan's high spiritual rank and influence as a scholar were intertwined with his devotion to his mother. He was widely respected not just for his knowledge but also for his character. His acts of prioritizing his mother over scholarly debates and work were a testament to his understanding of the true meaning of righteousness, which is why Allah elevated his status among the scholars of his time.

6. Fudayl ibn Iyad: From a Life of Sin to Elevated Spiritual Status Through Filial Devotion

Fudayl ibn Iyad, originally a highway robber who later became a revered ascetic, was also known for his change in behavior toward his mother after his repentance. When Fudayl decided to change his life and dedicate himself to Allah, one of the first things he did was to focus on serving his mother. He would sit beside her, take care of her needs, and express regret over his past transgressions. It was said that he would cry out of fear of having wronged her in any way during his days of rebellion.

Fudayl's deep remorse and subsequent devotion to his mother led Allah to forgive his sins and elevate his status as a saint and teacher. His story shows that repentance and returning to Allah also require making amends with those closest to us, particularly our parents. His elevated spiritual status later in life reflected Allah's pleasure with his sincere devotion to his mother.

7. Yahya ibn Muadh Al-Razi: Carrying Out His Mother's Desires

Yahya ibn Muadh Al-Razi, an influential preacher and ascetic, was known for his devotion to his mother, even in the smallest things. He would carry out her desires with joy and never show a sign of reluctance. Yahya was known to serve his mother with his hands, refusing to let servants do what he considered his responsibility.

Yahya ibn Muadh Al-Razi's devotion to his mother allowed him to reach a high spiritual level. His status as an inspiring preacher was linked to his sincerity and humility, cultivated through his devoted service to his mother. His story exemplifies how caring for one's parents refines one's character and leads to an elevated spiritual rank.

Summary

The stories of later-generation Muslims demonstrate that kindness to parents is a timeless virtue that holds immense value in the sight of Allah. Allah often rewarded their devotion to their parents, leading to increased knowledge, spiritual elevation, and widespread respect. The stories reflect that being good to parents is an integral part of attaining closeness to Allah, as it cultivates humility, patience, and unconditional love—traits cherished and rewarded by Allah.

The common theme across the stories is that respect and kindness toward parents do not end once one reaches a certain level of successor scholarship. Instead, success and elevation in status are often the fruits of sincere devotion to one's parents, both in their lives and after their passing.

Chapter 22

Kindness to Parents: Notable Examples from Contemporary Islamic Scholars

The examples of contemporary Islamic scholars being kind to their parents and earning a higher status due to their devotion are truly inspiring. These stories highlight how modern scholars continue to exhibit the utmost respect and kindness towards their parents despite the demands of their roles in education, leadership, and public service. Here are some notable stories:

1. Mufti Taqi Usmani: Prioritizing His Parents' Well-Being

Mufti Taqi Usmani, a highly regarded contemporary Islamic jurist from Pakistan, is known for his deep respect and love for his parents. He often shares stories of how his father, the esteemed Mufti Shafi Usmani, influenced his life. Even as Mufti Taqi Usmani became a respected scholar, judge, and teacher, he always attended his parents' service. During his father's illness, Mufti Taqi Usmani took care of him personally, balancing his time between his father's care, his scholarly work, and his responsibilities at the Islamic university.

Mufti Taqi Usmani's influence as a scholar and respected status within the Islamic world can be connected to his devotion to his parents. His father, Mufti Shafi Usmani, was also a scholar of high repute, and Taqi Usmani's dedication to his father's care exemplifies true filial devotion. The blessings he received in his career, his knowledge, and the respect he commands are, in part, a reflection of Allah's response to his service to his parents.

2. Shaykh Muhammad Mukhtaral-Shinqiti: Humility Before His Mother

Shaykh Muhammad Mukhtar al-Shinqiti, a contemporary Mauritanian scholar known for his knowledge of fiqh and hadith, often spoke of his deep respect for his parents. Despite being a highly sought-after teacher and scholar, Shaykh al-Shinqiti prioritized his Motherwell-being. It is narrated that he would not begin any of his public lessons or conferences without seeking his mother's permission. He would often share how her satisfaction was more important to him than the recognition he received from his students or followers.

Shaykh al-Shinqiti's dedication to seeking his mother's approval before major events in his life shows his recognition of the power of a parent's du'as and satisfaction. His success as a respected teacher and leader is a testament to the blessings that follow honoring one's parents. By placing his mother's needs above public acclaim, he showed that true success in Islamic scholarship comes not only from knowledge but also from earning the satisfaction of one's parents.

3. Shaykh Bin Bayyah: Compassionate Care for His Father

Shaykh Abdullah bin Bayyah, a prominent Mauritanian scholar respected globally for his knowledge of Islamic jurisprudence, has often shared his experiences caring for his elderly father. Despite his demanding schedule as an advisor, lecturer, and public figure, Shaykh Bin Bayyah prioritized his father's care, ensuring he spent quality time with him daily. He often credited his father's du'as for his successes, believing that the blessings he received were directly related to his devotion to his father's comfort and well-being.

Shaykh Bin Bayyah's global recognition, advisory roles to world leaders, and respect as a leading scholar of his generation are all, in part, blessings stemming from his devotion to his father. His story highlights that Allah elevates the status of those who honor their parents, even when they hold prominent public positions. His humility in prioritizing his father's needs over public duties reflects his understanding that true success lies in earning Allah's favor through dutifulness to one's parents.

Summary

The contemporary stories of Islamic scholars reveal a consistent theme: devotion to parents brings immense blessings and elevation in status. These scholars—Mufti Taqi Usmani, Shaykh Muhammad Mukhtaral-Shinqiti, and Shaykh Bin Bayyah—achieved prominence not only because of their knowledge but also because of their unwavering devotion to their parents.

Chapter 23

The Story of Jurayj, the Devoted Worshipper

The story of Jurayj (or Jurayh) is a well-known tale in Islamic tradition, illustrating the importance of obeying and honoring one's parents, especially the mother.

Jurayj was a devout worshipper of Allah who lived in isolation, dedicated to prayer and worship. He built himself a small monastery where he spent all his time in prayer, distancing himself from the distractions of the world.

One day, while Jurayj was deeply engaged in prayer, his mother came to visit him and called out to him, "Jurayj, your mother is calling you!" Jurayj, torn between continuing his prayer and responding to his mother, decided to remain in his prayer. His mother called him a second and a third time, but each time, Jurayj stayed silent, focused on his worship and did not respond.

After the third time, his mother became upset and prayed against him, saying, "O Allah, do not let him die until he sees the faces of prostitutes."

This was a serious supplication, and it was accepted by Allah.

The False Accusation

After some time, a prostitute from the village made a plan to bring disgrace upon Jurayj. She approached the village shepherd and committed adultery with him, becoming pregnant. When she gave birth to a child, she falsely claimed that Jurayj was the father.

The people of the village, outraged by this accusation, stormed Jurayj's monastery, tearing it down and dragging him out in humiliation. They accused him of fathering the prostitute's child. When Jurayj asked for the reason, they told him about the accusation.

Jurayj, remaining calm, requested to see the baby. He placed his hand on the child and, by the will of Allah, the baby miraculously spoke, declaring that the true father was the shepherd, not Jurayj. This miraculous event cleared Jurayj's name.

The people, astonished by this miracle, offered to rebuild Jurayj's monastery in gold as an apology. However, Jurayj refused and asked them to rebuild it like before—with mud and bricks.

Hadith

Abu Hurayra reported that he heard the Messenger of Allah (peace and blessings be upon him) say, "No human child has ever spoken in the cradle except for 'Isa ibn Maryam, may Allah bless him and grant him peace, and the companion of Jurayj." Abu Hurayra asked, "Prophet of Allah, who was the companion of Jurayj?" The Prophet (peace and blessings be upon him) replied, "Jurayj was a monk who lived in a hermitage. A cowherd used to come to the foot of his hermitage, and a woman from the village used to come to the cowherd.

The Lesson

The story of Jurayj teaches a powerful lesson about the importance of honoring and obeying one's parents. Despite his sincere dedication to worship, Jurayj's neglect in responding to his mother's call led to his temporary disgrace and suffering. This story emphasizes that fulfilling the rights of parents, especially mothers, is a vital part of one's faith in Islam, even for those deeply devoted to worship.

This incident is often narrated to remind believers of the high status of parents in Islam and the consequences of ignoring their needs or requests.

CHAPTER 24

LIVES OF THE HADITH NARRATORS: BIOGRAPHICAL INSIGHTS

1. Imams of Kutub al-Sittah (the six canonical hadith collections in Sunni Islam)

The narrators of the major hadith collections are some of the most influential scholars in Islamic history. Each of these figures played a pivotal role in preserving and transmitting the sayings, actions, and approvals of the Prophet Muhammad (peace and blessings be upon him). Here is a brief biography of the six major narrators of the Kutub al-Sittah (the six canonical hadith collections in Sunni Islam):

Imam al-Bukhari (810–870 CE)

Full Name: Muhammad ibn Isma'il ibn Ibrahim al-Bukhari
Title: Amir al-Mu'minin fi al-Hadith (The Commander of the faithful in Hadith)
Birthplace: Bukhara, modern-day Uzbekistan

Imam al-Bukhari is best known for compiling Sahih al-Bukhari, which is considered the most authentic collection of hadith in Sunni Islam. Born into a scholarly family, he traveled extensively throughout the Islamic world to collect hadith, compiling over 600,000 narrations. Of these, he included approximately 7,275 hadith (with repetitions) in his Sahih, carefully verifying each one based on strict reliability and chain of transmission criteria. His rigorous method set a high standard for authenticity. He spent the latter part of his life in Khartank, near Samarkand, where he passed away.

Imam Muslim (821–875 CE)

Full Name: Muslim ibn al-Hajjaj ibn Muslim al-Qushayrial-Naysaburi
Title: Sahib al-Sahih
Birthplace: Nishapur, in present-day Iran

Imam Muslim is famous for compiling Sahih Muslim, the second most authentic hadith collection after Sahih al-Bukhari. Like al-Bukhari, he traveled across the Islamic world in search of hadith and compiled around 4,000 narrations (without repetition) in his Sahih. His collection is known for its systematic structure and precise arrangement of hadith by topic. Imam Muslim was a student of Imam Bukhari, and their works are considered complementary to one another.

Imam Abu Dawood (817–889 CE)

Full Name: Sulaiman ibn al-Ash'ath al-Sijistani
Title: Sahib al-Sunan
Birthplace: Sijistan, in modern-day southeastern Iran

Imam Abu Dawood is the compiler of Sunan Abu Dawood, a collection of over 5,000 hadith. His compilation focuses on the practical application of Islamic law (fiqh) and contains many narrations related to jurisprudence. He was deeply committed to verifying the authenticity of hadith and often clarified which narrations were weak. He was a student of Imam Ahmad ibn Hanbal and traveled extensively to learn from hadith scholars throughout the Muslim world.

Imam al-Tirmidhi (824–892 CE)

Full Name: Muhammad ibn 'Isa ibn Sawrah al-Tirmidhi
Title: Sahib al-Jami'
Birthplace: Tirmidh, modern-day Uzbekistan

Imam al-Tirmidhi is best known for compiling Jami'at-Tirmidhi, one of the six major hadith collections. His work is distinctive because, in addition to narrating hadith, he provided commentary on the strength of each narration and noted differences of opinion among scholars on various issues. His collection includes around 3,900 hadith. He studied under many notable scholars, including Imam Bukhari, and his work remains highly regarded in both hadith and fiqh.

Imam al-Nasa'i (829–915 CE)

Full Name: Ahmad ibn Shu'ayb ibn Ali al-Nasa'i
Title: Sahib al-Sunan
Birthplace: Nasa, a town in present-day Turkmenistan

Imam al-Nasa'i is the compiler of Sunan al-Nasa'i, also known as al-Mujtaba. His collection focuses on the authenticity of the narrations, and he is known for being extremely cautious in accepting hadith. His collection is distinguished for its meticulous attention to detail, and many scholars regard his narrations as being highly reliable. In total, he compiled around 5,700 hadith in his Sunan, although he wrote other works as well, including a longer collection known as Sunan al-Kubra.for his He was known for his piety and died in Makkah.

Imam Ibn Majah (824–887 CE)

Full Name: Muhammad ibn Yazid ibn Majah al-Qazwini
Title: Sahib al-Sunan
Birthplace: Qazvin, in modern-day Iran

Imam Ibn Majah is the compiler of Sunan Ibn Majah, the last of the six major hadith collections. His collection contains around 4,000 hadith, but it includes weaker narrations than the other five collections in Kutub al-Sittah. Despite this, his work remains highly influential and is regularly referenced in Islamic jurisprudence and hadith studies. Ibn Majah's Sunan is particularly important because it supplements the other collections with narrations not found elsewhere.

The Legacy of the Six Collectors

These six hadith scholars collectively preserved the sayings and practices of the Prophet Muhammad (peace and blessings be upon him) in a way that would serve as a foundation for Islamic jurisprudence, theology, and ethics. Their rigorous methodologies, deep knowledge, and tireless travels to verify and collect authentic narrations have made their works timeless references for Muslims. The Kutub al-Sittah has been studied and analyzed by generations of scholars, ensuring the transmission of Islamic knowledge remains reliable and authentic.

Their contributions are central to Islam, and their works are studied worldwide to this day.

2. Other Narrators of Hadiths

In addition to the six major narrators of the Kutubal-Sittah, other significant scholars and compilers of hadith collections played pivotal roles in preserving and transmitting the sayings, actions, and approvals of the Prophet Muhammad (peace and blessings be upon him). Here is a biography of a few other important hadith narrators, focusing on those whose collections also have a significant influence on Islamic scholarship:

Imam Malik ibn Anas (711–795 CE)

Full Name: Malik ibn Anas ibn Malik ibn Abi Amiral-Asbahi
Title: Imam Dar al-Hijrah (The Imam of Madinah)
Birthplace: Madinah, in present-day Saudi Arabia

Imam Malik is best known for his compilation Al-Muwatta, regarded as one of the earliest and most authoritative collections of hadith and Islamic jurisprudence. Unlike other compilers, Imam Malik focused on gathering hadith and legal rulings specifically from the scholars of Madinah, believing that their practices were closest to those of the Prophet (peace and blessings be upon him) due to their proximity in both time and place. Al-Muwatta contains approximately 1,720 hadith and legal opinions, making it a foundational text for the Maliki school of thought in Islamic jurisprudence. Imam Malik's influence remains significant in Islamic legal theory, and his collection remains a key reference for scholars.

Imam Ahmad ibn Hanbal (780–855 CE)

Full Name: Ahmad ibn Muhammad ibn Hanbal al-Shaybani
Title: Imam of Ahl al-Sunnah (The Imam of the People of the Sunnah)
Birthplace: Baghdad, in present-day Iraq

Imam Ahmad ibn Hanbal is the compiler of Musnad Ahmad, one of the largest hadith collections. It contains over 30,000 narrations, categorized according to the names of the companions of the Prophet (peace and blessings be upon him). Imam Ahmad was a key figure in the preservation of the hadith sciences and profoundly influenced the development of Islamic theology and law. He was also the founder of the Hanbali school of thought. HisMusnad, while not part of the Kutub al-Sittah, is highly revered due to its vast coverage of narrations and the authenticity of many of its reports.

Imam al-Darimi (797–869 CE)

Full Name: Abdullah ibn Abdul Rahman al-Darimi
Title: Sahib al-Sunan
Birthplace: Samarkand, in present-day Uzbekistan

Imam al-Darimi is the compiler of Sunan al-Darimi, which, though not one of the six major hadith collections, is still a significant source of hadith. His collection contains over 3,000 narrations and is often cited by scholars for its reliability and attention to authenticity. Al-Darimi's Sunan is regarded for its focus on both the chain of transmission and the content of the hadith, making it a valuable resource for scholars of hadith and Islamic jurisprudence.

Imam al-Bayhaqi (994–1066 CE)

Full Name: Ahmad ibn al-Husayn ibn Ali al-Bayhaqi
Title: Imam al-Bayhaqi
Birthplace: Khurasan, in present-day Iran

Imam al-Bayhaqi is best known for his work Sunan al-Kubra, a comprehensive collection of hadith especially useful for Islamic jurisprudence (fiqh). He was a student of the Shafi'i school of thought and compiled hadith, emphasizing its legal implications. His Sunanal-Kubra contains more than 10,000 narrations and is often referenced for its detailed commentary on the reliability and meaning of each hadith. Imamal-Bayhaqi also authored several other works on hadith, including Dala'ilal-Nubuwwah (Proofs of Prophethood), a collection focused on the miracles and characteristics of the Prophet Muhammad (peace and blessings be upon him).

Imam al-Hakim (933–1014 CE)

Full Name: Muhammad ibn Abdullah al-Hakim al-Nishapuri
Title: Al-Hakim
Birthplace: Nishapur, in present-day Iran

Imam al-Hakim is the compiler of Al-Mustadrak 'alaal-Sahihayn, a hadith collection intended to gather narrations that met the conditions of authenticity used by al-Bukhari and Muslim but were not included in their collections. Al-Mustadrak contains over 9,000 narrations, some of which are highly authentic, while others have been scrutinized. Imam al-Hakim's scholarship is widely respected, and his collection is considered an important supplement to the major hadith works, even though not all of his narrations meet the same rigorous standards of Sahih al-Bukhari and Sahih Muslim.

Imam Ibn Hibban (d. 965 CE)

Full Name: Muhammad ibn Hibban al-Busti
Title: Sahib al-Sahih
Birthplace: Bust, in modern-day Afghanistan

Imam Ibn Hibban is the author of Sahih Ibn Hibban, which is considered one of the most authentic hadith collections after the six major works. His collection is unique for its strict methodology for verifying the authenticity of the narrations, focusing on both the chain of transmission and the content of the hadith. Ibn Hibban was known for his deep knowledge of hadith and was a pioneer in categorizing narrations into different chapters and themes.

Imam al-Tabarani (874–971 CE)

Full Name: Suleiman ibn Ahmad al-Tabarani
Title: Sahib al-Mu'jam
Birthplace: Tabaristan, in present-day Iran

Imam al-Tabarani is the compiler of three major hadith collections: Mu'jam al-Kabir, Mu'jam al-Awsat, and Mu'jam al-Saghir. These works contain thousands of narrations, with Mu'jam al-Kabir being the largest and most comprehensive. Al-Tabarani's collections focus on narrations from various companions of the Prophet Muhammad (peace and blessings be upon him) and are especially valuable for their breadth. His works are widely cited by scholars for their historical value, though not all the narrations are considered authentic by later scholars.

Summary of Contributions

These scholars and the narrators of the Kutubal-Sittah have played a monumental role in preserving the sayings and actions of the Prophet Muhammad (peace and blessings be upon him). Their collections are foundational to Islamic scholarship, especially in hadith and fiqh (Islamic jurisprudence). Their tireless efforts in verifying and categorizing hadith have given Muslims the knowledge to practice their faith according to the Sunnah of the Prophet (peace and blessings be upon him). The works of these scholars continue to be studied and revered across the Islamic world, serving as a timeless resource for those seeking to understand Islam.

Conclusion

As we come to the conclusion of ***Keys to Paradise: Serving Parents with Excellence—Forty Hadiths on Honoring and Respecting Parents***, it is clear that Islam places immense emphasis on the relationship between parents and children. Through the forty hadiths presented in this collection, we have explored the profound spiritual, moral, and emotional obligations that children owe to their parents. The Prophet Muhammad (peace and blessings be upon him) repeatedly emphasized that honoring and serving parents is a matter of familial duty and a key to earning Allah's pleasure and attaining Jannah (Paradise).

The teachings of these hadiths remind us that respecting parents is an ongoing commitment, one that does not end with their passing. Whether through direct acts of kindness, prayers for their forgiveness, or living righteously as a reflection of their upbringing, we carry their legacy forward, benefiting them and ourselves in this life and the Hereafter.

In a world that often moves quickly and prioritizes individual pursuits, these hadiths call us back to the timeless values of gratitude, humility, and compassion. Our parents are the gateway to our worldly existence and a means through which we can attain eternal success. The teachings found in these hadiths guide us to treat our parents with the utmost respect, care, and excellence, recognizing that their rights are vast and their sacrifices immeasurable.

As you reflect on these hadiths, may you be inspired to deepen your connection with your parents, whether they are alive or have passed on. Seek Allah's pleasure by honoring them, and may your dedication to their service be a source of blessings and rewards in this life and the Hereafter. Indeed, the path to Paradise begins at home, with those who nurtured and raised us.

May Allah grant us all the ability to serve our parents with excellence, earn their pleasure, and, in doing so, secure His mercy and the ultimate reward of Jannah. Ameen.

End Book Review Request

Dear Reader,

Thank you for exploring ***Keys to Paradise: Serving Parents with Excellence: Forty Hadiths on Honoring and Respecting Parents***. Your support and engagement mean so much to me. I hope the book has enriched your understanding and offered practical guidance for your personal and spiritual growth.

I would be deeply grateful if you could take a moment to share your thoughts on the book. Reviews play an essential role in helping others discover valuable insights, and your feedback can truly make a difference. Whether you post your review on Amazon, Goodreads, or any other platform, your honest reflections are greatly appreciated and will help spread this important message to a broader audience.

https://www.amazon.com/review/review-your-purchases/?asin=B0DKBRQ54W

With sincere gratitude,
Aisha Othman

References

- Abbasi, M. (2014). The Luminaries: Lives and Teachings of the Classical Scholars. Ta-Ha Publishers.

- Abu Dawood, S. (n.d.). Sunan Abu Dawood. Dar-us-Salam Publications.

- Ahmad ibn Hanbal. (n.d.). Musnad Ahmad. Dar-us-Salam Publications.

- Al-Adawiyya, R. (n.d.). Sayings and Teachings of Rabi'aal-Adawiyya.

- Al-Bukhari, M. I. (n.d.). *Al-Adab Al-Mufrad*. (Trans. S. Kahn). Darussalam.

- Al-Hakim, A. N. (n.d.). Al-Mustadrak.Dar-ul-Kutubal-Ilmiyya.

- Al-Islam.(n.d.). Biographies of Islamic Scholars. https://www.al-islam.org

- Al-Nasa'i, A. A. (n.d.). Sunan al-Nasa'i.Dar-us-SalamPublications.

- Al-Tabarani, S. Y. (n.d.). Mu'jam al-Kabir. Maktabaal-Ulumiwal-Hikam.

- Al-Tirmidhi, M. (2007). Jami' at-Tirmidhi (Vol. 1). Riyadh:

Darussalam. (Original work published ca. 884 CE)

- An-Nadwi, S. H. (1979). *Saviors of Islamic Spirit* (Vol.1). Academy of Islamic Research and Publications.

- Ibn Kathir, I. (1996). Al-Bidaya wa'l-Nihaya (The Beginning and the End). Maktaba al-Ma'arif.

- Ibn Majah, M. (2007). Sunan Ibn Majah (Vol. 5). Riyadh:Darussalam. (Original work published ca. 887 CE)

- Islam Q&A. (n.d.). *Hadith Database and Fatwas.* https://islamqa.info

- Muslim ibn al-Hajjaj. (n.d.). *Sahih Muslim.* (Trans.A. Siddiqi). Sh. Muhammad Ashraf.

- Muslim, I. (1971). Sahih Muslim (A. Siddiqui, Trans.). Beirut: Dar al-Arabia. (Original work published ca. 875 CE)

- Philips, A. B. (1997). *The Fundamentals of Tawheed(Islamic Monotheism).* International Islamic Publishing House.

- Rabbani, F. (n.d.). SeekersGuidance. Retrieved October 15, 2024, from *Reflections on Blessed Life & Gatherings of the Beloved Prophet Muhammad* https://seekersguidance.org/articles/prophet-muhammad/reflections-on-blessed-life-gatherings-of-the-beloved-prophet-muhammad-shaykh-faraz-rabbani/

- Sunnah.com. (n.d.). Islamic Hadith and Biographies https://sunnah.com](https://sunnah.com)

- Syalvi, A. H. (2004). Lives of the Salaf: Stories from the Golden Era of Islam. Islamic Book Trust.

- Usmani, M. T. (2002). *The Authority of Sunnah.* Maktaba Ma'ariful

Quran.Sunnah.com. (n.d.). *Authentic Hadith Collection*. https://sunnah.com

Made in the USA
Columbia, SC
01 November 2024